Feeling Red?
Blush ♡

Blush！♡

ISBN: 978-1-9995366-4-0

Hair and Make-Up: Kitty Doan
Photography: Kitty Doan (taythy77@yahoo.com)
Book Cover: Nazanine Nabizadeh
          (nabizadeh.work@gmail.com)

Glory Be

To

GOD

For

He

Is

LOVE

Lovers of love, expressionists of passion, recipients of adoration, objects of desire, witnesses to undying devotions...

Erlinda Caido Carolino
Aubrey Delima
Gina Delliper
Toni Dicastri
Angela Hansen
Judi Leemhuis
Katrina Madarang
Teresita McLaughlan
Norma Pollock
Ann Strong

Anonymous

A heartfelt thank you for sharing your letters of love.

A Very Special Thank You to the Translators:

Ivy Edad
Ginalyn Mendoza
Patricia Naguiat
Grace Openshaw

Blush!

"Putting together this collection was such a thrill! It certainly gave me an emotional high, complete with giggles and smiles. So, get your blanket, put your feet up, snuggle with a cup of hot cocoa, and allow this book to softly caress your whole being." - Me-An Laceste

TABLE OF CONTENTS

There Must Be A Way 1

My Wife, Jean.. 2

Unrequited Love.. 3

Summer Moon On The Beach............................. 7

WSWAK (Was Sealed With A Kiss) 11

Kissin' and Huggin' 13

Radio.. 15

Mah Honey 17

Phonograph 20

Electricity and Magnetism 23

Aubrey, The Rock 27

Win/Win.. 28

I Love You Because...29

Sunshine Girl.. 32

Beautiful Valentine.. 36

A Secret Relationship 37

Till The End Of Time 38

Say You Love Me 40

Please Tell Me... 41

Only Death Can Stop My Loving You 43

My Girl.. 45

Bleeding Heart... 47

Linda.. 49

My Dearest Love...50

Under Your Spell 51

Lorelie...53

Undying Devotion 55

The Comfort Of Your Love 58

What Medicine You Are 61

Heart And Soul...64

Yours Completely 66

You Will Be Mine...68

Warm Embrace 70

You Mean Everything To Me 72

Usual Thing For Lovers 74

Rumours Of A Secret Relationship 76

Sweet And Tender Love.....................................78

Remember, You Are My Teacher!....................82

No One Knows...83

Am I Your Problem?...85

Did She Read The Letter? 86

Forgive Me...88

What Kind Of Girl?..89

I Will Have To Tell My Sister 92

Confession 94

Secret Marriage 96

Jukebox...98

Your Girl 102

'Ling 104

Martial Law 106

She Knows 108

How You Honour Me! 109

I Want You To Be Proud Of Me 111

A Date With My Friend 115

Abu...117

Blast-Off..119

Lucky Charm 122

Answering Machine..124

Been Courting You 126

Couldn't Get Through.......................................129

Strange Empty Feeling......................................131

I Can't Bear Not Knowing 133

I Would Not Have Let You Go 135

So Upset At Leaving You 137

I Only Wanted To Be With You..............................139

You Did Not Wish To Marry Me 141

A Bottle Of Wine..143

It's Not Worth Being Away From Home................145

Dimples..148

Nothing Happens By Coincidence 149

Long Distance...151

Perennial Seeds 154

Fortune Cookies 155

Fissure and Fault...158

The Perfect Song..162

Feeling Red?
Blush ♡

THERE MUST BE A WAY

There must be a way, to help me forget that we knew

There must be a way, to stop me from dreaming of you

There must be a star, in the skies that reflect your eyes

I just don't know how to disguise, how much I miss you

There must be a song, that doesn't remind me of you

There must be a kiss, to thrill me, like yours used to do

I look for a way to be happy, happy with somebody new

Oh - there must be a way, but I can't find a way without
you

John Francis B.
July 1990

My Wife, Jean

A little about my wife Jean - Jean Mary B. She was the most wonderful mother in the world - the mother of Ann, Martin, Gerald, Wendy, and Susan - who she called her baby. They all loved her very deeply. She will forever be remembered for her love and affection to them and by her husband, whom she called Jack. She will be remembered for the tolerant way she handled difficult situations during the bringing up of her children. The endless patience she exercised during the adolescent period, which can try the best of us.

Many incidences occurred during her lifetime, the greatest of which was the 1939-1945 war. 6 years is a lifetime for family life to exist without the help of her husband, but Jean was made of the material that is in so short supply today; hence the marriage survived some 52 years.

She will never be forgotten by the family and moreover by her husband.

Until we meet again - Darling XXX.

Jack

April 1990

November 2017

Dear V,

I haven't been able to say this to you the way I want, but I love you so much. I knew the first night we met that God had brought you into my life for a reason. We have known each other now for just over 6 months. I have been through a lot of personal struggles these past 6 months, but you've made every moment together my favourite moment.

We just had a large talk about this relationship and what we both want out of it. I want to be in a committed relationship, and you don't. You want your space and freedom. Part of me is struggling with this a lot. I can feel insecurities and jealousies coming up, but there is another part of me, too. One that knows this is exactly what is supposed to happen before we are together. It may be a little painful now, but it won't matter because we are supposed to be together.

You and Me. On Friday you said you hope it's me and you in the end. As soon as you said that, I saw our whole lives together. I couldn't tell you about it at the time, because it wouldn't have landed the same way. I'll tell you one day though. I saw us together. I saw us getting engaged and married; the moment I tell you I'm pregnant and when we have our first baby. I saw us at Christmas visiting my family, and I saw us travelling to

3

India. I saw us growing old together, laughing and kissing.

You said those words, and everything in my life up until this point made perfect sense. And everything I've seen that was blurred became clear. We are going to have the most amazing life together. We are going to have so many adventures. I think that's what makes right now hard. I have to be patient and let you go through what you need to be ready for me. Because this is it.

You are who I have been waiting for. I already love you more than I can describe. You are such an amazing man. I don't think you realize how special you are. I knew from a young age the man for me would be very successful. Not just in business, but in all aspects of his life. I knew he would be strong and kind and loving. I've been looking for this man my whole life and somewhere between May 8th when we first met, and now, I realized he was you.

You are everything I'd been praying for. You aren't perfect, but you are perfect for me. I love your smile and your big dark eyes. The way you hold my face and kind of squish it when you kiss me. I love your sense of humour and how you think you are the funniest man on earth. I love your hands and how you wrap your big arms around me when we sleep. I feel so safe in those arms. I have never been attracted to another human being the way I am with you. You are intoxicating. I love how smart you are and how you are always striving to grow and develop yourself. I love how big your heart is.

I can see how much love you have to give and how you try so hard to make me happy, even when you are conflicted. I am going to try my best over the next few months to be supportive of you and give you the time you need. I am going to enjoy this time I have for myself. I know I don't have to worry. I know you love me even if you can't say it yet. In the grand scheme of things, this will feel like a second, and I should savour it. You are amazing. I've wanted this a long time, a little bit longer will be ok.

Until then, I will love you and keep those words safe in my heart. Until you are ready to take them from me.

Yours,

T

Jean Dear:

You did not want me to say I love you. You do not want me to write it. But it's your birthday. All-day long you will be in my thoughts. I will be seeing you in my each moment as you were so dear and lovely when you let me kiss you good-by. You don't know how blue your eyes are and how gold your hair. There's no other girl in the world who's sixteen today and beautiful as you are.

Did you ever feel you were on your knees to another person and wanted to be there? That's the way I feel about you, Jean. Please do not send me back this bracelet. It would mean you do not want to remember the beautiful time we had together. I'm not sending it, Jean, with my remotest thought of holding you. I send it only for remembrance and because the days we had are precious, though there never came the like of them again.

I did not ask if you wanted my picture, I can not explain why it seems so important that I should send it. Perhaps in the hope that you will look at it once in a while, think of me and long to meet again under a summer moon on the beach – we shall, Jean, we shall.

You are dear to me. You are very dear. You will always be.

Forever yours,

Jack

"Jack passed away one year after he has written this letter to Jean. His life was cut short at a tender age. However, he must have been a remarkable young man as this letter was kept tenderly away in a small special box together with their photo. It was then passed on to the care of Jean's daughter-in-law. Jack left a beautiful legacy in Jean's heart and mind. I wonder, did she ever imagine what could have been their love story?"

Feeling Red?! Blush !♡

"Mom first saw Dad when he was recruiting for WWII. He performed in an acrobatic army group all over Saskatchewan. The group would perform and then have a dance and then sign up men and women volunteers for the army. He next served overseas, all over Europe and was among the group who liberated Holland. When he got back home, he and his brother, Jim, started a "Lunch Counter/Cafe" called the "The Ho Boy" in Saskatoon. At that time, my Mom was at nursing school in Saskatoon.

One of the other nursing students was Teddy Jones, who was dating my Dad's brother, Jim. They lined up my Mom and Dad on a blind date. That was truly the beginning of their romance. Mom went back to the small town of Milden during semester breaks and studying times before tests so they would write every day. These are some of my Dad's "love letters". I wish I had Mom's letters to him. Mom was always happy with my Dad, and they had a long and successful marriage, raising 5 children along the way.

They were married from 1948 until 1997, just one year shy of 50th anniversary." - Judi Leemhuis

Ho Boy Service
Saskatoon, Sask.
Friday April 11th, 1947

Hello Honey:

Received your lovely letter yesterday (1:00 a.m. now). Thank you! I must say that you have me quite spoiled 'cause I look forward to your letters and expect them. But regardless don't you slow down any.

I sure have not caught up on my correspondence. If I tried I'd be writing two or three hours after I finish yours! And that would not do, would it? Possibly this week-end I may get a chance.

Yep Jim has been baking some more pies. Still has difficulty with the crust. Yesterday afternoon Teddy was over and baked some cup-cakes and pies. Turn out pretty good too. The batch and pies made last Sunday didn't last long. Ten of them went Monday and the rest on Tuesday.

So you won't be able to drive into Saskatoon aye? That's bad - terrible, terrible, terrible! Seems like six months since I've been out with dat little rascal, Haddie. Sure got to do something about it. Them sox is a good idea. I don't think it's a bribe. So don't worry - you may knit me a couple of dozen pairs size 11! How's that?

Today we received a new addition to our abode. A police pup. He's a cute, smart dog. Gonna train him to be

11

a good watch dog. He limps a little on one rear leg so naturally I named him Limpy. Couple of nites ago John went out the back and there outside was a cigarette butt still burning, so someone must have been snooping around. A good watch dog would come in handy. The psychological aspect of a big Police dog would put the fear into any ordinary person.

Notice by your letter that you had rain out your way. No rain to speak of here but - last nite and this morning we had scads of snow. Great big fluffy snow-flakes were tumbling down. The ground was pretty mucky during the day.

Well my dear it's five minutes to two and I still want to wash my hair so methinks I ought to conclude 'til next time. There's enough to bore you now. Incidentally have you got that $5000.00 yet? I'm lonesome.

Good Nite now & Sweet Dreams.

With love and kisses,

Same ol Bill.

P.S. WSWAK. WY

Dear Haddie,

Must say that I was elated to receive your letter today. Sorry, I cannot keep up with you, but however, I'll make up for it in another manner when you get back. Darn it, you should have been here by now, presto-like!! By the way, how much of your vacation will you have left when you return to Saskatoon? Better make it about a week aye?!! Remember that I have to catch up on some kissin' and huggin'! You're such a musher that you are way ahead of me, you little Rascal.

Say that is quite the drawing you have on one of your letters. What gets me is that even when you are away, you seem to know what I look like. But there is just one little thing wrong, you got my ears a little bit too long. Guess you didn't want to be too perfect!

What do you mean how could I stand it? Two months isn't long enough, in fact. There is a saying, patience is a virtue. People like to be virtuous. So that's what they have to have lots of to put up with me!!! You'd be surprised if I told you how many faults I have, so I won't.

Jim and I like your clippings, especially the one where one can learn to cook during a long telephone conversation. Think I'll have a portable phone installed.
Thanks for the snap too. I'll send one which I think the most difficult we had to do. Lovely scenery too, aye?

Well, Honey, think I'll close for tonite. Hope you're fine and the rest of the family too. We are O.K. here! Business pretty good these days.

Good nite and sweet dreams.

Love 'n Kisses

Bill

P.S. WSWAK *(was sealed with a kiss)*. WY

Hello Honey:

Bet this letter may be a slight surprise, 'cause I just suddenly felt like writing a short letter to my honey. Sure cannot seem to settle down to doing anything properly. A horribly lazy character I am.

Hope that your trip back was enjoyable and that the rear end of the car did not suffer too badly from all that baggage. Your dad sure took a chance with his car?!?!

Seems like you have been gone a long time! Must be nearly finished with your studying now. I am already looking forward to your return. Ought to be back in a week aye? And I do not mean a week from the 15th! If not, guess I'll have to go out there!

This afternoon I took the slab of bacon and the remaining piece of cottage roll to Ludwig's and had it sliced. Before I left, they had supper ready, so I had to stay for it. I'll be getting fat starting the week off with a big meal. Oh well, I can get back to my diet tomorrow.

Teddy is over now, and is studying. They had supper together and looking at them made me feel darn lonesome! Incidentally, Jim and Teddy saw a card up

15

town so they are sending it along. And Teddy says that Pat Roberts looked lovely at her wedding last night.

Speaking of last night, I had a horrible time. Jim and Teddy went to a dance. Olka went bowling, and I went to the radio. Was wishing I had a phonograph and our record to listen to. However, by a strange coincidence, I heard "Clare de Lune" on the radio, and its sweet strains made me feel a little better! Am I not an awful sentimentalist?

You sure looked lovely tonight. With that lovely smile, you look just like a beautiful rose! And remember you always have a smile!

Well, Honey, before I completely bore you with my chatter, time maybe to close. Hoping you are fine, and best regards to the rest of the family.

Bye now,

Lovingly,

Bill

My Dear Honey:

Jeepers here, it is 10:30 and I am just starting my letter to you. Jim and I just got each other insured for $5000. The salesman just left so here I am, honey.

Sure like your letter. It arrived this morning. Looks like it's a letter a day. However, when I received a letter from mah, honey, I just got to answer it even if it was 3 AM. You know why? You don't? Well, I'll tell you when I get to Milden.

You asked about those ball games. Yours' truly was losing 'till the last game. Between three people, I bet $2.25. So I'm up bout $1.25. I'm luckier on ball games than bettin' on rain it seems!!??

Say that's tough about Birdie's folks moving away soon. She's a very nice girl as I could gather from my first impression.

Doris and Murray are together again. What a couple of characters! Life sure is complicated.

Dave is fine. Edith had a touch of the flu last few days. But they expect to leave this week-end for Edmonton. Then Dave will return to work. Dave was over tonite and bought some choc. bars and a pound of peanuts. Do you like peanuts?

Teddy is over tonite. Studied a bit and fell asleep while us mugs were talkin' business. Teddy says that one of your patients, Holstead, had his operation yesterday, but they cannot do anything for him due to the fact that the dura has adhered right to the brain as a result of a former haemorrhage. (Cats what lingo!) oh yes, Teddy says that they finally got Young to work for two weeks on staff.

I see your morning hours are irregular. You lucky rascal. Don't tell me that there is still some of that bacon left. Sure wish I could bring some-more. Our supply here is very small and no near future supply it seems. Guess it'll be more eggs, beans, etc.

Jim and I changed our system of earning cigarettes, slightly. On top of the former agreement, we will also draw a pack for a $90 day. Today was only $89.24 darn it. Our other objective is over $114.00. We are doing a lot of rolling these days.

How is the weather out your way? Been gettin' any rain recently? Should have 'cause it blew dust galore and sprinkled some. It better be nice this week-end!! I hope! I hope!

Teddy didn't go to that wedding. Just heard about it. So she did not acquire any pointers.

18

By the way, Jim and I done somethin' today. Teddy was a little surprised. That's something else I'll have to tell you when I visit mah honey.

Al must be havin' quite a time. He had better hurry up and sell that new car of his, before its value depreciates.

Dog-gonnit, every time that radio here plays sweet music, I get horribly lonesome. Aren't you finished with those books yet? Ought to be here by now!! Just now, there was some lovely Hawaiian serenading, m, m.

Sweetheart, I'd better close for tonite. Gotta get up early, and I still have to shave tonite. Two days crop on my fiz. Jim worked out in front today. Oh yes, Jim didn't get up in time with the result we were both up at 7:25 AM. Should have seen us swish. Had coffee made in less than ten minutes.

Oh yes, I was going to close, so, good nite, dear.

With love,
Bill

P.S. kiss, hug, hug! WY

Dear Beautiful:

Sure sweet to receive another one of your letters today. You know honey every time I am graced with one of your letters, it makes me feel better!

During the afternoon I heard "Clair de Lune" over the C.B.K. (radio). It was sure good and made me think of the times at your place when we sat together listening to it. There I go again, just an old sentimentalist. But I cannot help it, unless I keep them to myself!

Business today was horrible. At least so far and there's only a half-hour left. However, that's the way she goes sometimes.

Jim already had completed his letter to Teddy, then he jumped into our 1948 Limousine to mail it and take Olka home at the same time, but he got as far as Olka's 'cause the fog was too thick, and considered too dangerous going up town so I'll mail his and this letter at the same time.

Have my honey's letter out in front of me to answer all queries.

I see those uniforms of yours are quite a problem. Maybe that is the cause of the depression of your feelings. If I have any bearing in that respect, then this weekend will be of mutual advantage. If I can get down. Will try to make it sooner than five hours.

Glad to hear that your dad and mom had a nice trip.

You said it; I sure like "Begin the Beguin." Will have to get me a good assortment of records and a combination radio and phonograph (automatic).

Oh yes, you wanted to know what I did Wednesday nite. Why that's the nite my honey called me long distance. It was lovely! And I wrote my honey a letter the same nite. Thursday nite, Technocracy and same old thing. On Nov 4th, there's a speaker from Vancouver who will address the public.

Teddy and Jim agreed to write at longer intervals so as to give her more time to study. By the looks of Jim's letter, it is no 16-page epistle.

Sure glad to know that you like my letters. I think they're awful 'cause I certainly take a backseat when it comes to writing. Lack of education, I guess. Wish I could write as good as my honey!!

Well, my sweet, I will terminate my jabber for this time. Check to make sure this letter gets to Milden tomorrow and mail both letters.

M.M. you sure look lovely!!

Good Nite Hon!

Love,

Bill

P.S. How's the studying? Ought to be finished by now!!! WY

Friday June 11th, 1948

Sweetest Adelaide:

You're such a lovely girl, and you send such lovely letters. Every time I read them, they make me tingle inside. And you know what it is - you don't? ... well, it's that electricity and magnetism, and it's even in your letters. And I love it!

I'm sure glad tomorrow is Saturday 'cause I'm going out to see my honey. This boy is gettin' so lonesome, and he is losing his composure as the day is drawing nearer, and the excitement is gradually overcoming his will power! Yipe! Won't it be lovely when it's all over, and we are comfortably settled? A beautiful, exciting wedding, a glorious honeymoon and starting life anew, a young, optimistic couple, my honey and I!!!

Jordan was over just a moment ago. Soon as the paper came in, he started to look for a suite. He and Jim went to look at one at Leland Court 203 E No. When they got back, they said that the suite is poorly furnished, and coal-oil permeates the air. I presume that by the time they are married, Jordan should find a place to live.

Last nite as I was going out the front door a chap in a car hollered at me. I got the car and drove up alongside. He told me his name was Mike Derwores. He said that Bill received the invitation and intends to drive down for the wedding. Mike was taking a '40 Plymouth to Edmonton for their brother Tony who is a radio operator at Fort St. John. They have a five-piece orchestra at Kamsack, and he said that Bill has cancelled some engagements to go to Milden.

After the meeting at the Section, I took six beers up to Mike's room. He finally got one in the Empire. So we drank and talked a lot. Mike had been married to a French girl from Winnipeg. Now they are separated. He said that he'd only gone out with her four times before they got married. Sure looks like that was inadequate.

The other evening I heard "Clair de lune," it sure sounded nice and magic-like. Beautiful like my sweet honey!

You know what? It's only six days then our big day. Gee, honey, it's sure gonna be super.

My sweetheart, if I want this letter to catch the Rosetown train, I'll have to swoosh now. So, I'll close now with loads of love and hoping everyone, 'specially ma honey, are fine!!

Yours lovingly,

Bill

P.S. I Love You!! XO. WY

Feeling Red?!
Blush ♡

September 14, 2019

Aubrey,

This is a fun experience. The first funny thing was when I had to stare at some stranger in the eyes for a few minutes. The only other person I did this with is you. When it was my time to stare at you, I looked at you and remembered how beautiful you are like the time I said my vow to you. You've changed to become a beautiful person inside and out. You have been an inspiration to a lot of people. You are my rock. I need you. Our family needs you, especially the Delima's. You have made our family closer, made us have somewhat of a dialogue with my parents and brothers. I luv you for that. You should be proud of yourself.

Greg D.

September 16, 2019

Aubrey,

I was thinking all morning today about our seminar on the weekend. Mostly about win/win situations. I did not realize that I have one in front of me. You wanted me to come with you to this seminar because you believe that I would benefit from it. But from me wanting to get a refund that would make this a lose/lose situation. Also, I should just accept the gift you chose and not refunding it. This will make it a win/win. If I did not graduate with you this Wednesday means we did not complete this together like you wanted. I should take risks to change my programming. I realized that it's a little change, but if you're willing to drop 6 bills, I should, too. You do the finances anyways. Yesterday I could not find any ways of implementing what we were talking about in my everyday situations, but there it is. I am slowly understanding. I WON'T ask for a refund, and I ACCEPT your gift. If I love you and thank you means I love myself and thank myself. That's pretty deep. I love you.

Greg D.

September 29, 2017

Darling –

It's here! It's here! Our wedding day is FINALLY here!! This day is 325 days in the making (yes, I counted, are you really surprised?). And after 9 months of daily FaceTime calls, roughly 32,000 miles travelled (yes, I also calculated that), approximately 97.5 adventures, and way too many good-byes, today marks the day that we officially start our lives together.

Five days ago, you and I stood on a start line for the Ironman and I've been thinking of how many parallels there are between a race like that and a marriage - the hard work, the empowerment, the team spirit, and a "finish line" that makes everything preceding it worth it. This little race we're starting now doesn't have a finish line but I know there will be so many steps along the way that make challenges worth it. So, as we stand on a new start line this morning, let's first look back at the last 325 days and marvel at the fact that we not only grew to know each other intimately in that time, but we also grew together enough to fall in love. Then, let's look forward and celebrate the fact that we have a lifetime and eternity to keep growing to know and love each other in ways that we can't even comprehend!

I met with a church leader a few weeks ago and he shared one final piece of advice that I've been waiting to tell you until today. He said that saying "I love you" is

29

great, but learning to say "I love you because..." was far better. So, Darling, I love you BECAUSE...

... you have a hunger to learn and try new things and to teach me new things. Nothing is off-limits for us in our adventures, except maybe dogs.

... of your ridiculously handsome smile, your funny faces, and your light-hearted spirit that helps me not to take me or my life too seriously.

.... you so obviously long to have a family. You will be an amazing father and I seriously cannot wait to start that phase of our lives together (okay, maybe I can wait a tiny bit).

... you are so comfortable around me and I can be my true self around you - no make-up, unbrushed hair, baggy t-shirts, burping - and I still feel beautiful. We can be vulnerable and completely at ease.

... everyone speaks so highly of you! That may sound like a weird reason to love you, but it shows your character. You are who you are to everyone you meet, and everyone loves that person.

.... we've learned we don't always agree. We have opinions and passions and we like to talk about meaningful, substantive things. And we're always able to work through things and figure them out together.

... you support me and have my back. You want me to fulfill my biggest (and smallest) dreams and life callings, whether they be jobs, moving, training, etc. And I want the same for you.

... and finally, because you love me unlike I've ever been loved before.

I love you because of all those things and more, some of which I don't even know yet. So, let's walk boldly and confidently today (and perhaps a little giddy), and stare the future and all of its joys and challenges in the face. Let's continue to have each other's backs no matter what. Let's promise to always do the small things. Let's have some fun celebrating with family and friends. And, most importantly, let's promise each other and our God that we'll give this thing everything we've got! Bring it on.

I love you today. And forever.

Your soon-to-be wife

14 March 2006

Paul, every so often I look over at you and I take a
moment to really see you – see you in your element doing
your thing and being yourself, completely focused or lost
in thought – and I absolutely love you. I have no idea how
the future will play out and what we will decide down the
road. I'd like to keep you in my life and keep loving and
doting on you forever, but for now we only have today
and I cannot know what tomorrow may bring. We must
live in the moment and do all in our power to make the
most of NOW. That will set the foundation of future
happiness no matter what might come our way. Whether
we end up together or go separate ways I love you. You
have had a profound affect on me and my life for which I
am very grateful. We have grown together and supported
one another through many diverse hardships and times
of great joy. I desire to see the world with you and explore
all aspects of life with you by my side. Your love has
sustained me, your confidence lifted me, your admiration
inspired me, your constancy comforted me, your support
strengthened me, and your trust improved me. I truly am
a better woman for loving you. I love you with all my
heart and you know how much I want to continue to be a
part of your life. Never doubt my love for you, even when
I'm mad. I am beautiful just for you.

Your Sunshine Angel

Feeling Red?! Blush ♡

"Roger was in his last year of medical school when he stopped. His mother, through his father's service as a Philippine soldier during World War II, was receiving a pension from the United States Army Forces in the Far East (USAFFE) until she remarried. Without other financial resources to finish his education, he looked for a job and was offered a teaching position away from his hometown.

His dormitory was inside the school compound, and outside its perimeter stood the only convenience store within the area. That's where a young girl, named Lyn, worked when she wasn't at school. Her father and sister owned and ran the business.

With the friendship developed amongst themselves, he would sometimes get invited to dinner, especially on days that his salary was spread thin between him and the 3 younger siblings he was supporting. In return, he would tutor Lyn on her math homework, where he, himself, was the teacher. She was at that time, in the North American Standard, in Grade 9.

Roger was 15 years older, and Lyn looked at him and treated him like an older brother."

His

🖤

Letters

Linda dearest,

I want you to know that I am delighted that you did not fail me, my beautiful Valentine partner. I am indeed very sorry for the thing that I had done. I do hope you can understand and that you can forgive me for what happened. From now on I promise to please you and to never do anything that will hurt your feelings.

You know, Linda, you mean the world to me, and God knows how much I really love you. May the Valentine card remind you always of me, someone who is crazy about you. My heart beats for you. My lips call for you. My eyes want to see only you. Your beauty has charmed me, and I am under your spell.

Happy Valentine, Sweetheart.

Forever loving you,

Roger

19 February 1971

Lyn dearest,

Once again, I want you to know that you are the girl I have chosen to be my life partner. So, please have faith and trust in me the way I have faith and trust in you. I do love you. Please believe me, my darling. I am willing to do all the things that you want me to do. Anything to make you happy so that you will never regret loving me.

By the way, you need not worry. Our relationship will remain a secret. I beg you to please be careful so that nobody will know except the two of us. At least for now. We can enjoy our love just between us.

Dear, if you do love me, too, please reply to my letters as soon as you are able. The days in between are too long, and I miss you very much. It will certainly make me so happy to receive letters from you, and I look forward to them coming and reading. It's my connection to you.

Study hard and take good care of yourself. Be a good girl.

Forever loving you,
Roger

23 February 1971

Dearest Lyn,

The serene call of life for me is to love you. I will not tire of whispering the words your heart longs to hear. I love you very much, my darling.

You are always on my mind. I feel restless being away from you. I feel uneasy when I could not see you. I tremble with excitement when I know that I will see you. You may not believe me, but God knows that I am telling you the truth.

My darling, I have sworn before God a promise, that I will love you till the end of time.

Lyn, I pray that our differences will not be a hindrance to loving each other. We are all created equal in the eyes of men and of God. Do not worry about these so-called differences. We shall work on overcoming them, learning from and supporting each other. We will grow even closer when we work together, so let us bind our hearts with love so strong that only death can separate us from each other.

You are my hope and my inspiration. Without you, my life will be worthless and meaningless. In your hands lies my fate, so please hold me and be my guiding star.

My darling, please let me know your likes and dislikes so that I can adjust. Would you like to know my likes and dislikes, too?

Bye dearest.

Forever loving you,

Roger

P.S. Please answer me, my love.

3 March 1971

Lyn dearest,

I beg you, my dearest, to please let me feel the comfort of your love. Why, until now, you have not said that you love me, too. I need your love to give me hope and inspiration. I want facts and evidence from you through notes and reply to my letters. I hope you will not fail me.

Lyn, do your family and friends already know about me and my pure intention towards you? Please let me know so that I know what to do to keep our relationship secret until that very day when the two of us will kneel at the altar and proclaim our love before God, our family and friends, and promise to love each other till eternity.

Please let me know what is going on before I leave for Bohol.

Forever loving you,
Roger

P.S. Kindly please reply to me as soon as possible. This is my special request to you, my darling. It will be wonderful to have your letter to keep me company on my travel.

14 March 1971

Lyn, my love,

One more time, I would like to let you know that I love you so very much. I am ready to marry you any time you want to prove to you my purest intention. I offer you my love that is genuine and sincere.

If, however, there is no place for me in your heart, or if you think I am someone who is not worthy of you enough to love, or that you can never learn to love me, no matter how excruciating the pain is, I will accept it and the heartache wholeheartedly. Perhaps this is the fate written in the palms of my hands.

My love, so that I am not going to get tremendously hurt, while it's still early, please be honest and tell me if there's hope for me or not. I am begging you. I am pleading for your answer, and I am prepared to suffer the bitter tears that will come should you crush on my already bleeding heart.

Hoping and waiting for your answer. I hope you will not break my heart, but if you do, there's nothing I can do but to suffer my unfortunate destiny.

Forever loving you,

Roger

P.S. My dearest love, even if you will not return my affection and devotion, I will not change. I want you to remember that even when you don't see me anymore, I will still love you for as long as I live.

Goodbye, my sweet Lorelie.

Always and forever
loving you
till the end of time - R

Translated by: Ginalyn Mendoza & Me-An Laceste

Lyn dearest,

It is not very easy to be living away from each other. I missed you so much, my darling.

I always pray to God, with fervent hope, that you will never change. May you always remember those happy moments we shared together. Lyn, I love you, and God knows how much and how much you mean to me. I really care for you. I made my vow before God that only death can stop my loving you. However, if I am no longer worthy in your sight because of what I have done, please tell me the truth. You said to me before I left to not disturb you anymore. Do you really mean that, my darling? Don't you love me anymore?

Even if it pains me so much, if you tell me that you don't have feelings for me, I ought to accept the truth and must resign to my fate. I will be willing to suffer for it if, in fact, it is the truth, but I hope it is not.

I want you to know that I will go on forever loving you. My love for you will never die. I will never forget you, my Beloved. As long as I live and though it will just be memories, I will make those memories of our love alive and will be my only consolation in my life while I suffer the pains and agonies of my broken heart.

I shall nervously await your reply.

Forever loving you,

Roger

National Media Production Center
D. Plaza, Alaminos
Pangasinan

5 October 1971

Lyn dear,

Ever since you have said yes to me, I do not know how to describe my feelings. You made me the happiest man in the world. I will make sure you will not regret being my girl. How could I do anything but to make you happy ? You are the most precious treasure of my life. There will be no other girl for me but you and that I promise you with all my heart and my soul.

Although we started as friends and also as your teacher, I am glad that now we have an understanding. I could not contain my delight knowing that you have feelings for me, too. I am so happy that it has changed from looking at me as a big brother to now as a boyfriend.

Every night has been restless thinking about you. Sleep was elusive because of the uncertainties I had about your feelings towards me. I prayed that you will look at me with love in your eyes, and now that my prayers have been answered, you cannot imagine how fast my heart has been beating even as I write to you now. Tonight, I will sleep with a big smile on my face and in my dreams, you and I will be holding hands because we cannot do that yet in public.

I am over the moon for being officially your boyfriend and you, my girlfriend, but, I want to share with you and your family the sorrows in the passing of your grandmother. My sincerest condolence. May she rest in peace. Let us take everything to God in prayer for comfort during this time.

Since I started my work in the government, it seems that we have not stopped moving around. We are very busy going around the first district of Pangasinan, gathering news reports and knowing the condition of the people. But despite being busy, I think of you always. Wherever I go, you are there with me because you are safely tucked in my heart.

Forever loving you,

Roger

P.S. Please reply to my letter, my beloved. I cannot wait to hear from you. I want to hear how much you care for me.

Lyn dear,

Before you completely forget the memories of our love, please allow me to express my feelings for you.

Lyn, as I contemplate the situations that became witnesses to our love, until now, I can not believe that you can forget me just like that. I almost came to the point of losing my mind and can not imagine that you could ever forget me because when I decided to love you, I gave my whole heart to you, Lyn. I gave my promise. My undying love for you knows no end. It is forever.

But now, it seems that my pure love is bound to be forgotten due to reasons I do not even know, nor do I understand. Lyn, if forgetting me is what you really want, my dear, I will accept my misery. I will be deeply hurt, but if it makes you happy, I am willing to sacrifice and endure the endless pain to make you happy. I hope that you will succeed and achieve everlasting joy in your life. Despite my pain and suffering because of you, I will always pray for your eternal happiness.

Even though I have bestowed upon you my faithful, sincere and pure love, to you, it is still worthless. I will go as far away as possible, so there will be no chance of seeing you again as it will just be unbearable.

Before my bleeding heart leaves you, my lips shall say it once more, that you are my greatest love even if you forbid its happiness. My heart is broken into a million pieces because it has offered you true love. My affection, if you only have the compassion to really see, is reserved only for you. I thought that you know, that you can feel, that you can see, that I love you and adore you. I will never forget the memories of our love. It is etched in my heart and mind forever. You may leave me, but the memories of you shall stay with me.

Goodbye, my love, I will go away suffering in exchange for your happiness. I wish and always pray to our Almighty God for your success and endless joy.

Always and forever loving you,

Roger

Note: Enclosed in this letter are two poems I wrote for you.

LINDA

My source of happiness is you
so I hope, my darling, you will understand
the pleadings of my crazy heart
I will love you till death do us part

If indeed my affection is just foolishness
by all means, punish me
but I will say it again, only you
I will love forevermore

When I fell in love with you
I offer my endless devotion
this heart of mine is preserved only
for you, Lyn, whom I have made promised to

Because of you, my darling, I shall forget
all the difficulties and all the sadness
you are an inspiration I shall not forget
thank you thank you to our loving God

Expect that I will love you
and trust that I will adore you
you are loved, you are thought of
and I will love you even more until my last breath

Translated by: Me-An Laceste

My dearest love,

My love for you has no end
nothing can compare to my love for you
you are the one I care deeply
the only one my heart beats for

even though I am far from you, my love
I will not change forever and ever
my heart is reserved only for you, Lyn
the girl I gave my promise to

you are the one who taught me
to charm you, and to love you
you know that you are the girl
who inspires me in this challenging world

you are the twinkle of my lonely heart
the light that I use in the dark
my search for your presence
is proof of my pure love

my only prayer to God
is to bless our lives together
and when the end shall come
let God welcomes us in His care.

Forever Loving you, Roger.

Translated by: Patricia Naguiat & Ivy Edad

Lyn dearest,

Darling, I am so happy to know that you do love and care for me, but the more I will be pleased if you do love me because of what I am and not because of the helping hand I had extended to you. I do hope sooner or later you will learn to love me because of who and what I am.

Lyn, I understand your situation, but if you sincerely love me, you have nothing to worry about if they will find out about our relationship. I know they will understand if we will explain and tell them the truth. Whatever will be their decision after knowing about our relationship, do not worry, I will not change. You know I am under your spell. I also know that God will not forsake us; instead, he will abide with us and see us through.

I want you to know that because of you I am working very hard for our future. Deep in my heart, my greatest concern in life is your eternal happiness. I will do my best to make you happy and to achieve my goals of supporting your dreams. So, darling, let us work together to build a strong foundation worthy of our future children. Let us encourage and inspire each other.

In God, I trust everything hoping and wishing that my dreams in life will come true; that you and I will live together till eternity because I will go on forever loving you. No matter how busy I am, you are always in my mind. You may be far away from me, but you are safe in my heart.

Always and forever loving you,

Roger

National Media Production Center
4th Floor GSIS Building
Dagupan City
3 March 1972

Lyn dear,

How is my sweet and ever dearest Lorelie? I do hope you are in good health and beautiful as usual.

Dear, I am proud to let you know that your darling is one of the two personnel in the regional office of the National Media selected to train as radio and telecom operator for 6 months, all expenses paid with salary plus overtime and allowance. My schedule is from 2:00 PM to 10:00 PM. Although it is quite challenging, and we always finished later than the scheduled time, it is fascinating, and I enjoy it very much. I usually arrive home from Dagupan to Lingayen at 12 midnight, very tired.

There are times when I feel that the strenuous training is hard for me to handle to the point of utter physical and mental exhaustion, but the very thought of you gives me inspiration, strength, and encouragement to do my very best. You see, honey, for you I will do anything and everything because I want you to be happy. We will have a good start when the time comes that I claim you for my own, and I am yours forevermore. If there's one wish I can make, it is that our love will last a thousand lifetime.

My dearest, what are the comments of your family and friends? Have you told them about our relationship? Do they like me? Accept me? Are they angry at you? Us? Please let me know. It is my prayer that they think of me as a good enough man for you, someone who cares for you deeper than any ocean. Please let me know what their reactions are.

Bye for now, my love. I really miss you. I hope and I can't wait to see you really soon. In the meantime, know that I am always thinking of you.

Always and forever loving you,

Roger

National Media Production Center
4th Floor GSIS Building
Dagupan City
16 March 1972

Lyn dear,

I arrived from a business trip to Alaminos (Philippine National Bank) last Wednesday when my office mate handed me your sweet reply. You cannot imagine how delighted I was to read your messages of love, but I was also concern about your well-being.

My darling, may I advise you to try and be cool and be calm with whatever they may say regarding our relationship. Trust everything to God in prayer, hoping that someday they will give us their understand and blessing. You need not worry. Let us prove to them that we are really meant for each other, not just here on earth but in the eternities, too. Try to relax, be understanding, and rational in handling their criticism. Don't let things affect our goals and the sincerity of our love. Concentrate on your studies and prove to them that their dream and expectation of you shall not be in vain. With focus, it will be realized and will come true.

Let not difficulties and frustration alter the intensity of your undying devotion to our cause, for the building of a beautiful and happy future together. The harder the toil, the glorious is the triumph for beyond the thick dark clouds, the sun is shining.

My dearest, I want to let you know that I will not tire of waiting for you. Please promise me that you will never change, that my waiting shall not be in vain. I beg of you, my dearest, if it is not too much to ask, and if you truly love me, let us marry secretly to ensure ourselves to each other. To get married will be proof of our sincerity to our love and with each other.

Also, I want to hear from you words that say you really love me, too, vowed with a promise that you are mine forever. I hope you can understand me. Let us make a promise that we will never part. Will you promise to be true to me as I am true to you?

Well, I think I have gone on too long on this topic. Let me tell you what is going on in my work. We were in Hundred Islands last Saturday with the beautiful ladies of Secretary Cxxx. At least that's what my colleagues say. I did not notice. There is only one beautiful girl for me, and that is you, my sweetheart. At one point, I was left alone in Lucap before we proceeded to Anda at about 8:00 in the evening. It's where we had our dinner. Then back again to Alaminos to join Sec. Cxxx and Vice-Governor Sxxx, who were the speakers fo the Alaminos Captains' League and the crowning guests of Mona Barrio Fiesta in Alaminos. Sunday, March 12, we were in Anda and Cabungan. Even with two nights without sleep, I arrived in Dagupan Monday morning and reported to my duty very very sleepy. I was all alone in my little room, and the temptation to fall asleep was strong.

So that you know where I am our upcoming schedule is as follows:

March 19 - Alaminos and Burgos
March 24 and 25 - Bolinao
April 1 - Tondol, Anda
April 2 - Bolinao

All of these are for fiestas. It is so busy but exciting and enjoyable. I hope to see you on April 1st. So here goes the news. This is your one and only signing off till the next mail. Sweet kisses and sweet dreams, my love.

Always and forever loving you,

Roger

Note: I haven't received the Valentine card you sent to me in Alaminos, but I will try to verify this at work and at the post office as soon as possible.

3 April 1972

Dearest darling,

Amidst the pressure of our nonstop travel schedule and with sleep catching up with me, I try my very best to respond to your letter, which was handed to me before the Holy Week. I feel so happy, in spite of my tired body, as I read your letter once more. Yes, darling, because I have known now the comfort of your love. I am also relieved to know that your sister already knew about and understand us and our situation. I hope and pray that the rest of your family will have the same understanding.

As for me, despite all the hardships and difficulties, I am inspired by your promise. You give me hope and inspiration to carry on with my job. You know, darling, I was assigned to arrange the itinerary of the secretary and so wherever he goes, I go with him, too. March 25, we were in Agno then went to Anda at about 11:00 pm. We left Anda almost as soon as we got there to go to Lingayen. Sunday, March 26, we went back to Agno and visited some of the remotest barrios (villages). At about 9:00 pm in the evening, we proceeded to Bolinao to attend the Ilog Fiesta. We stayed there until 12 midnight then went to Lucero in Santiago Island because the secretary was to crown the winner in their town fiesta. We left Lucero at about 5 am then went to Bugallon and Aguilar to attend to some important business. At about 8 am, we left to go to Bauang, La

Union and then to Baguio, where the secretary met with the President. I went back to Dagupan to report to my job and stayed in the office until 10 pm. I reported for my duty from Monday until Good Friday.

Last Saturday I was with the secretary, and we attended the Tondol Barrio Fiesta. That was when my colleague and I dropped by at your store to buy cigarettes. Your brother and Elias were there, but you were not. From there we met the secretary in Catubig at 7 o'clock to go to another barrio fiesta in Alaminos. We were there until 5 am. From there we went to San Fernando, La Union, where we slept and only for two hours. We went back to Anda, Sunday afternoon, and got there at 6 pm. Lack of sleep and an exhausted body did not deter me from wanting to see you, so I went to your house to visit you and hopefully get a chance to talk to you privately as I have missed you so much. Unfortunately, you have visitors, and my time was very limited. Oh, how I want to spend even just a brief moment with you, to hold your hands in mine will be enough to sustain me in my difficult job. I was very disappointed not to have that opportunity.

My colleagues were about to leave when I got to our place from your house. We immediately left to go to Bolinao and were there until 3 o'clock. After the coronation, we left Bolinao to go to Baguio for the conference of all the cabinet members and then I went back to Dagupan to report to my duty until 11 that night. When I got home, my body wanted to go straight to bed, but my thoughts are of you. I don't think I will have a good sleep without responding to your letter, so here I am, writing to you even when I could hardly keep my eyes open.

I hope you don't tire reading my detailed update about what I have been doing. I want you to know that no matter how busy and exhausted I get, that you are always in my mind. You are the reason why I can do what I do. Your love gives me strength.

By the way, we will be there again on the 21st and 22nd of this month. I really hope we can talk then, my love. Your darling is very sleepy now, and so I send you sweet kisses before closing my eyes. I love you.

Always and forever loving you,

Roger

Dearest Sweetheart,

Due to our hectic commitments from April 2 to May 2, I was not able to respond to your letter at once. So, I beg you, my dearest, please understand me and my very busy work. I hope you don't get impatient waiting for my reply.

I want you to know that your image is emblazoned in my mind. Wherever I am, and wherever I go, you are there with me. Please believe my promise that my love for you will never change. God knows how much I love you, and how much you mean to me. You are my everything.

You know, darling, I am always out with the secretary. Wherever he is, I am there with him. I have not even reported to our office since April 20. That day we went to so many towns I was up the whole night.

The next day, even without sleep, we went to San Fernando, La Union, only to come back later to Anda to attend a varsity night and spent two nights here. On April 23, after we left your store, we proceeded to Binabalian as an advance party. If you only knew how on that day, we were like a headless chicken running here and there and with just about an hour of sleep. The following day we left very early to go to Baguio to meet the President.

If I write all the details of our comings and goings, you would feel dizzy just by reading it. Sometimes I wonder how I, and the rest of our party, manage to survive the grueling ordeal of working with the secretary. We eat on the road most of the time, but what I longed for is a good night's sleep on my very own bed and, of course, to be with you and hold your hands.

I don't even remember anything special about my birthday on May 1. We were out all day that day attending so many affairs, including the meetings of the ABC (Association of the Barangay Captains). I finally was able to drop by our office the next day before heading out to yet another road trip. Your second letter was then handed to me. I wanted to read it right away, but I couldn't, so I safely put it in my shirt pocket. I would like to have a quiet moment with your letter and with you.

I got home at past midnight, and no matter how sleepy I was, I opened your letter and found a birthday card and two pictures of yours to greet me on my birthday. Thank you, my darling, for making my heart jump with joy. What medicine you are for my tired body! I hope to send you my latest photo as soon as possible. I will be with you on your birthday, May 19, 1972.

I am looking forward to having a private moment with you to talk and plan for our future.

Sweet kisses, my darling. I will see you and embrace you in my dreams.

With love and care,

Roger

Dearest Sweetheart,

On your very special day that is coming, I have nothing extravagant to give you as a birthday present, but I offer you my heart and my soul. I pray for you, your safety, happiness, and good health. Darling, although we are far apart, my thoughts are filled with beautiful thoughts of you. I hope you remain forever sincere and faithful to our love as I am.

Last Tuesday, May 2, 1972, I thought I could have a little rest, but one of our personnel had an accident, so I had to attend to him and was responsible for relaying his condition to his family. I barely slept for one week. I was then assigned to our patrol unit to cover the news while he is confined to Nazareth hospital. And then when I was supposed to have a day off last Sunday again, I was sent to cover the news of the fire that hit Agoo. That same night we were in close watch for the patient until he died. So, can you imagine from May 8 to 14 we were busy, and sleep was a luxury? After the funeral on the 14th, I was assigned in the patrol communication going to Manila and back to Dagupan. One week straight of day and night service, but I must respond to my duty. It's a difficult life, my darling. I hope you are enjoying it for me.

What a week it has been with the death of a colleague and a terrible fire. I am looking forward to having a nice break when I see you on your birthday.

Too tired and sleepy, but I want to send you my love before I close my eyes.

Forever loving you,

Roger

24 May 1972

Dearest darling,

As usual, your letter gives me joy and happiness. I'm so sorry, however, that I was not able to come for your birthday. It was my eager and fervent desire to go and celebrate it with you, but time did not permit me to do so. I know you understand the nature of my job. I hope I did not hurt your feeling, but if I did, please condone me my darling. Although I was not able to come, I prayed for your happiness and wishing you the very best.

I want to congratulate you as the new assistant registrar. This is truly a double celebration. More power and wishing you to enjoy your new vocation.

How was the celebration? Did you prepare cakes for my coming, darling? I am sure you did. It's just so unfortunate that I couldn't come.

Oh, Before I forget, what has Miss Cacho told you about my past? Does she still remember Me? Tell her that I will never forget her.

What was the reaction of your sister when she read my letter to you? Was she happy? Was she upset? Please let me know.

As for me, despite my hectic world, I am enjoying my work. Imagine my work from Monday to Sunday. That is every day. There is no holiday at all. Aside from my own work, I was also assigned to cover all the engagement of Secretary Cxxx every time he comes to Pangasinan.

Last Friday, we went to Baguio for his speaking commitment. We stayed at the Pines hotel. Saturday, we went to Cabanatuan and then back to Dagupan. Sunday, we were on the road again, visiting so many towns until we were back to where we started at 4 o'clock in the morning. We are repeating this same routine again on Friday. Can you imagine travelling so much with little sleep?

So goes the news. Your darling is signing off. Till the next issue of my travel report. Bye and best regards to all. Good night.

Always and Forever,

Roger

Note: Keep me in your thoughts always until that very day when I am yours completely, and you will be mine till eternity. Missing you so much, darling. I hope and pray to see you soon.

National Media Center
4th Floor GSIS Bldg
Dagupan City

28 June 1972

Lyn dear,

It seems that the long silence has temporarily drifted us apart. I hope it does not mean the end of our beautiful love. If only you can look into my heart. You will see your angelic face painted there. My heart beats for your love. My hands yearn to hold yours. My body longs for your embrace. My lips crave for your kiss. I know I have not written to you for a while, but you are always on my mind, my ever-dearest sweetheart. Please forgive me for my neglect. My work seems to have taken over my every waking moment and even sometimes when half asleep. At the end of the day, I could not even hold a pen from exhaustion. I hope you can understand how busy my world is.

What keeps me going are your sweet tender words - my inspiration and my guidance. I work very hard for my promotion and transfer to the Voice of the Philippines Radio Networks, which will open a branch in Alaminos by July. I am hoping that by August I will be a staff member of that same branch. Pray for it, darling, and be my inspiration in preparing for our future. I want you to be happy when that very day comes when you will be mine, and I will be yours forever in the eyes of men and of God. I don't want you to regret loving me and being called Mrs. Erlinda Cxxx Cxxx.

I understand you are busy too in your work both at home and at school. Is that why until now you have not answered my last letter? Please please find the time to respond to this letter. I really want to hear from you as I missed you more than you will ever know.

Always and forever loving you,

Roger

Note: Please let me know when I can see and talk to you. If possible, Saturday, which is supposedly my one day off in a week. I need you, honey, and I will be waiting for your reply.

Lyn dearest,

May the best of everything abide with you always through the guidance and blessings of our Heavenly Father.

Dear, may you have peace of mind in everything you do. Take it easy and take good care of yourself. You have nothing to worry about, and you need not worry about me. Just bear in mind that you are the one I love. You are the one I care about. You are the one I need in my life. Be patient, honey, be brave in facing our challenges, especially with being away from each other. Let us have faith that everything will be okay. In the meantime, let us work hard to reach our goals.

As for me here, through the blessings from above, I am doing fine. I am doing my very best and saving for our future and our happiness' sake. So, darling, if sometimes I fail to send news from me to you, I beg of you to be patient and give me your understanding.

'Ling, after my last visit with you, I left for and stayed in Manila for one week. From there, I went to Baguio to attend a conference and stayed there for a week also. I was lucky to represent our branch in Dagupan. It has been enjoyable, but it would be more enjoyable if you were with me, my darling. Baguio is foggy in the morning and cold. I will not need a sweater if I am wrapped in your warm embrace. I do pray and hope that someday soon, we will enjoy the best of everything in life together.

So, there goes my news, my love. I am now signing off until the next letter.

Always and forever,

Roger

20 December 1972

Lyn dearest,

I wonder why until now you cannot trust me and do not have confidence in me. You treated our love as if I am nothing to you. Is it because I am not your true love and that you are only forced to love me? Before it is too late for me to find that your love would be unkind, please let me know the truth so that it will not torture me when one day you are gone, my love.

My dearest, if you think I cannot make you happy for I am not the man for you, please don't be afraid to tell me. Though it will hurt with unbearable pain, I am willing to set you free to look for a man worthy in thy sight, who can own you completely and have your trust and confidence. I want you to be happy.

Please know, though, that when the time comes when you remember me no more, I would still be loving you as my love for you will never die. It will go on till the end of time.

Darling, you may change, but my love for you will linger. You may forget me, but I will go on forever loving you. You may deceive me, but I will remain faithful and sincere to you. You may doubt my sincerity, but I trust you and have faith in you. I may be nothing to you, but you mean everything to me.   You may turn unfaithful to our love, but I promise and vow to be true to you.

Dearest, I have said everything to prove that you are my everything, but if after all these, you still doubt my sincerity and not trust me at all, then I leave everything in your hands. My fate lies in your decision. If you don't love me anymore, then do the things that will make you happy. For the sake of your eternal happiness, I am willing to suffer and sacrifice. If you want me to set you free, then your wish is my command. I will go and will never bother you again. I will be out of your sight forever.

Always and forever loving you,

Roger

My Beloved,

Please let us forget our quarrels, forgive each other, and let us make a fresh start. Sometimes a small thing can get blown out of proportion, but I know our love is so much bigger than anything that comes in our way.

Lyn, forgetting you is the very thing I cannot do because you have become a part of my life. There will never be another woman for me but you because you are my joy, my life, and my everything. You expressed your worries about me forgetting you. Vanish this doubt from your heart and instead let the flame of our love burn from within you.

I have tried so hard, my dear, to prove that you are my everything, but you are always questioning me. Deep in your heart, there is fear that is causing you not to trust me. Is this the kind of love you are entrusting me? If you really love me and really sincerely love me, I beg of you to please have faith and trust in me.

I understand you and will always do my best to understand you, my dear, but it seems that understanding me is quite difficult for you. I know the very thing you are afraid for me to do. I will never do it to you, with you, until that day when we exchange our vows and when we bind our hearts as one. I understand that you are afraid, but this is a usual thing for lovers to do. However, I respect you and honour your decision.

My beloved, to avoid this particular trouble, I must go away and not bother you about it. I do hope that by so doing, you will have peace of mind. Please advise me on what to do to not hurt you. You know, dear, our office is waiting for my decision about the transfer either to Baguio or Zamboanga. If you think this is the only recourse to get out of this situation that you are afraid of me to do whenever I come to visit you, then so be it. I want to let you know that your decision will be my decision. I want you to be happy and not worry so much about it. I will be waiting for your choice of my assignment.

This is your beloved signing off.

Always and forever loving you,

Roger

P.S. Happy Valentine, Sweetheart.

22 March 1973

My Beloved,

Learning about the rumours spreading over there, it is my hope that you will not be bothered by it. If you really love me, darling, have faith that everything will turn out fine. Please bear in mind that as for me, there will never be another girl. There's no one else but you. You have captured my heart, and it is yours forever-more.

I promise to you and before God that nothing and no one can part us till the eternities. I pray that God's everlasting love may abide with us, reminding us to be faithful and true to each other.

Lyn, my dearest, I'm glad to inform you that I had just received my permanent promotion as assistant administrative officer at the NHPC regional office, Dagupan City. At the same time, I was offered an item in the GSIS Dagupan City. It is possible that with this new position, I get a much higher salary than what I am getting now. If everything materializes, I will then be ready to settle down for the fulfillment of my promise to you and of our dreams. I pray and hope that everything will be okay with you as well as your loved ones.

Dear, I want to know your plan so that I can help you to carry it out. If you have any problems, please let me know. You have nothing to worry about as I am always behind you, supporting and encouraging you.

I will be seeing you soon, possibly on your graduation day, to talk about your plans and finalize it if necessary. Confer and discuss it with your father and especially with your sister, too, so everything will be ready when I come. I pray and hope everything will go alright and smoothly.

Till then. I am now signing off. My best regards to you and your family.

Forever loving you,

Roger

My Beloved,

I know that deep in your heart, there is a doubt with regards to my sincerity. Why else would you be quiet? I can not bear your silence. Did you think I have forgotten you? That is not possible, my love.

Forgive me if I met your silence with my own, too, before this. I needed time to get rid of sad feelings that seem to happen each time we are together lately. Being together seems to me to do more harm to our relationship because we fight about trust. I do not want to have any more fights, so I decided to remain silent, just for the time being, even though it hurts. Maybe the short absence will make you miss me and realize how sincere I am to you. I hope you understand my purpose in doing so.

So, my beloved, can we work on getting rid of all those unworthy things and thoughts that might trample our otherwise, sweet and tender love? Let us enjoy our relationship without hurting each other's feelings.

I am indeed very happy to know that you are back in school now. Study hard and strive to make your dreams come true to help "our" dreams to come true. Let us prepare for a happy and successful future together.

Bye, my dearest. May God be with you and keep you safe.

Forever loving you,

Roger

Note: I will soon be seeing you, my darling. I do hope that you have found in your heart to give me your complete trust so that instead of quarrelling, we can enjoy our rare moments together.

I have been designated as a Provincial Coordinator and researcher, so I will be on the field on most days.

Feeling Red?!
Blush ♡

Her

🖤

Letters

February 21, 1971

To you, Sir,

I know the reason why you are doing these things. You are persistent because you already know that I am very close to you. I behave the way I behave because I consider you as one of my elder brothers, who are kind enough to help me with my math homework and other schoolwork. You are like a guidance counsellor as you give me advice when I have problems.

Sometimes I think that you are just tempted, but I do not understand why. Why me?

Sir, you must remember, you are my teacher, and I am only your student. If you will analyze it and see the picture, there is a significant imbalance. Please think and consider your actions. As a friend, I do not want you to have regrets one day.

From me.

7 - 5

To you,

Understand me, please. I can not give you an answer yet. I have not made a decision. Before I accept your love, I must really think first and consider if it is good or bad on my part. I need some time to think about this matter, especially that no one can help me or give me advice on what to do. Even my own sister, who is very close to me, does not know. You were asking if my parents and friends know – no one knows what is going on between us except you and me. I am not sure about your friends. Do they know? Please, kindly do not tell them.

I feel so nervous about what I am doing that sometimes my body trembles. I am keeping things from my sister, but I know I am not doing anything bad or wrong. As you know, she and I are close, and I feel that I am not being honest with her.

My reason for wanting to keep it a secret is that I do not want people to look down on you. You are a degree holder, a teacher, and I am a nobody, a mere student. Although you say that we are all created equal in God's sight, still, I am shy and do not feel confident enough to be your girlfriend. Besides, what will people think about our age differences? Please let me think about what to do and what my decision should be.

I know that you will be going to Bohol for two weeks. I hope you will enjoy your trip and that it is successful. Do not worry about our JS Prom. I will keep in mind your advice and follow your words to guide my way.

Lastly, my prayers will go with you to Bohol. Have a safe trip.

From me.

7 - 5

April 7, 1971

To you,

Do you have troubles? You seem to be carrying a heavy burden on your shoulders. I worried when I saw you looking like that. Will you share them with me so I may be able to help? Or, perhaps, I am your problem. Am I?

Please do not get hurt or offended if I am not able to write to you or reply to your letters immediately. I have so many school assignments and household chores, too. Besides, we talk at school even though as your student and as you, my teacher. By the way, I wrote you a letter before you went to Bohol, but unfortunately, it was too late to give it to you. I could not find you, and then I heard you left already.

You were asking me for a picture. I couldn't go to a photo studio yet, but I will make sure to go so it is ready for next time.

Until here. Always take vitamin "U."

Lorelie

Translated by: Me-An Laceste

May 18, 1971

Dearest Roger,

How is my dearest one this time? I hope that you are in good health.

I came back from the barrio yesterday. When the nighttime came my sister gave me your letter which was already open. I was very nervous, but I did not dare to ask her about it. She also did not say anything. So, I don't know whether she opened the envelope or not or if it was delivered already opened. I don't know if she tried to read the letter and the card.

Thank you by the way for the birthday card enclosed.

As much as I am thrilled to receive your letter, I was also shaking inside with worries. Many questions came to my mind: Does my sister know about you? Did she read the letter? Does she have any suspicion? Is she okay if I have a boyfriend? Is she okay if it's you? My mind could not stop thinking, but I went on pretending like she handed me something unimportant. For now, I will just be quiet unless she confronts me.

I also received another letter from you last week, but I was not able to respond because of too much work. I read in that letter that you are coming for my birthday. I am very excited to see you. I feel very special that you are coming on my birthday.

Dear, I started working in the office of Mrs. Carranza from May 1st, as an assistant registrar. Miss Cacho is my companion, and she is fond of telling me stories about your past. I am getting to know you more from her.

I have to go, so I will end my epistle now. Until the next mail.

I remain,

Lyn C. Caido

January 4, 1972

Dearest Roger,

I thought I upset you for not granting your wish. I regretted it, but you must also understand my side.

Dear, if in fact, I offended you, I am so sorry and please forgive me. I did not really mean to hurt your feelings. It was not my intention, and I do not want you to think our promises have come to nothing. It is my fault, and so I apologize. But, if this pleadings of mine will be ignored and forgiveness is not granted, I will not get angry with you, my love. Although it will hurt me more than you know, there is nothing I can do.

Do what you think can make you happy. I want you to know, though, that I never betrayed you nor turned unfaithful to you.

Hope you can understand me. And again, I say, please forgive me. Bye...

With you forever,

Lyn

88

Asbury College
Anda, Pangasinan
January 19, 1972

Dear Roger,

    With hopes and prayers that you are in good health upon receiving this letter of mine.

    As for me, I stayed in bed for more than one week, from January 4 to 12. I only went back to school and attended my classes last January 13, and our exam was on the 14th and 15th. I felt then that I still could not go, but I did not want to miss our examination. Maybe it was through your fervent prayers why I recovered faster. Thank you very much for that if you did so.

    Yes, I received your letter last December and another one today. I understand every line. But why do you still need to go to faraway places? You know what I mean. Yes, it is all my fault. I understand why you feel you have to go away, and I am the one to be blamed. Please do not do it. Maybe you say to yourself, "What kind of girl is she? She cannot remember all the helping hand I have given to her." But you are mistaken. The truth is, I am always thinking of all those help you have given me and the happy moments we have shared. Honestly, I am very
grateful, and I will not take your generosity for granted. However, as you can observe, I am still dependent on my father and on my sister, especially. So, I am really very

89

afraid to hear anything from them, anything related to our relationship. I have to be careful and must keep it a secret. It is necessary to keep it between the two of us. At least for now. I hope you can understand my situation at home. My father and sister are concern only about my future.

One thing more, last December 31, Friday, I was alone in the store, and while I was cleaning, I happened to see a letter in the corner of my eye, and it happened to be yours. It was your letter dated October 14. I found out that they have captured it. But I did not ask my sister about that letter and pretended I never saw it. I put it where I hide all the other letters. I was quite nervous, thinking about what they might say. I could not sleep that night. I tossed and turned just waiting to be scolded. I don't know if you have sent any more letters besides this one.

So, I advise you not to write to me all the time. I prefer for you to come to the store once in a while than to send letters. That is if you have enough time. They know you as a friend, so they will not suspect anything. I hope. But if you are busy because you are also working part-time in Great Plebeian, I do understand.

Let us be careful with our actions in the meantime.

So long for now.

Forever loving you,

Lorelie

Dear Roger,

I am glad to know that you are one of the two personnel in your regional office selected to train as a radio and telecom operator. Before going further, I hope and pray that you are fine as usual. I am fine, too, just in case you are wondering.

Dear, I can imagine how busy you are in your work after reading your letter. It makes me feel better to know that in spite of the difficulties you encounter, that you are, at least, enjoying it. Please be careful and take care of yourself. Please do not overdo it so you will not get sick.

I received your Valentine's card, but I doubt you have received my Valentine card and my letter. I mailed it last 22nd of February, and I addressed it in Alaminos when I thought you would still be there. Can you ask your co-workers from if they received any-thing from me? Otherwise, the envelopes should have been returned to me.

I want you to know that I appreciate your words of advice which inspire me in my studies. I will keep it close to my heart to serve as my guide since you are away.

Our family circle does not know yet about our relationship, but sooner or later, I will have to tell my sister. I am planning and thinking about what the best way is to open up, heart to heart, so that she will understand and accept us. I pray that she will.

So long... until next mail for more news.

Forever loving you,

Lyn

Note: Please do not write or sign your name "ARCE" in your mail. Thank you.

March 9, 1972
9:30 pm

To my only one,

Just what you encouraged me to do, I did my best to confess everything to my sister. It is regrettable, however, that she is not able to understand us or maybe because she was shocked to hear about you and me. She also read your letter but nothing. It did not help with her reaction.

I wonder why she could not be more sympathetic and sensitive. She must know what it must be like because she has fallen in love before, too, and at that time, I gave her my support, my understanding, and my listening ears. You know about this story.

It is my hope that one day she and the rest of my family will understand us and our relationship, that is if you can still wait for the day when I finish my schooling. I know that this is the reason why they are so worried about me. They are very strict and have given me so many rules, so I will graduate first before getting into any serious relationship.

Till here. I hope you understand, too.

94

It's me just the same.

Forever Loving you,

Lyn

Translated by: Me-An Laceste

March 23, 1972

Dearest Sweetheart,

Last Monday I left my place at 1 pm. I decided to walk to save some fare money even though it was hot and dusty. I arrived at 2 pm in Poblacion, all sweaty and tired, but when I reached the Asbury campus, Fely handed your letter to me. All of a sudden, my energy came back. I have forgotten all about my tired feet and instead settled in to read your message.

What a surprise it was? Did you envision what my reaction would be?

I understand what you wrote. You're asking if we could secretly marry to prove that I really love you. If you could only imagine how nervous I was to think about the very idea of getting married at this time, even if it is a secret? My mind rushed to consider what might that possibility look like, no, not about getting married, but what will happen if it was found out. My hands went cold, and my whole body started to shake as if I was convulsing. I am very sorry, but I could not do that, get married to you in secret. It's not that I do not love you, but I know the hardships and sacrifices of my sister in supporting me and putting me through school. I would feel so ungrateful to her when I know she works hard for me. I would feel that I betray her trust, and I do not want to do that, especially now that she knows about you and me and already understand and have accepted our relationship. I can not do it, my darling. Please remember that I do love you very much but understand my position on this matter.

You told me that you will not be tired of waiting for me. I promise you your wait shall not be in vain. My promise will be your proof of my undying love. I am faithful to you, and my love for you is sincere. You are my first love, my only love, and the last love of my life.

By the way, it's the Foundation Day at school, and last night was the beauty contest. However, we were not able to watch it because we went to Sablig to attend the wedding of Jaime Cxxx to our second cousin Gloria Cxxx. They are both studying at AI.

At present, the school is in high spirits in preparation for the coronation tonight. I don't think I can watch that either as I am left alone in our store. Tomorrow will be the parade as usual.

Until here. Remember, I love you.

Yours forever,

ECCaido

April 11, 1972

Dearest Roger,

Greeting you in God's precious name.

Your letter was handed to me last Friday (7th). I am pleased that you respect and understand my decision regarding your proposal. Thank you for your understanding. Let us do our best to always give that understanding to each other and build a strong foundation from that.

Dear, last April 8, we went on an educational tour in Manila for our zoology class under Mr. Rochs. We left Poblacion at 3:00 am, but we were delayed in Catubig until 6:00 am. We stopped in Sta. Barbara for breakfast at 9 am. We arrived at Serum and Vaccine Laboratories in Alabang, Muntinglupa, by 2:00 pm. However, we were not able to enter because we did not have a permit, so we left and at once proceeded to Taal Vista Lodge in Tagaytay. Again, Mr. Rochs thought it was free, but we were asked to pay 2.00 pesos each. Guess what we did? You are right. We left to find a place where we can see the view of Taal Volcano for free.

We also dropped by the Union Theological Seminary in Dasmarinas. It was the graduation of Pastor Caalim. While there, we also saw your uncle Pastor Caracas. At 7:00 pm we left the Central Church for our free time. Eme, Rita, Ruthie, Tony and I went to Pasay and had our dinner there. After eating, we went to Luneta until 12' midnight. A country girl like me in a big city I felt very much out of place, but nevertheless, I had a wonderful time with friends. Manila is so alive, even at midnight. As you know, in the country it gets quiet as people settle in when it gets dark and by 8 pm you would think the whole neighbourhood is asleep. Not there. The way people are going about, you would think that it is broad daylight.

Early Sunday morning, we left to shop in Pasay and returned at 10 am in time to cook for our packed dinner. After cooking, we visited uncle but only stayed for 5 minutes because by then, it was 11:45 am, and we were supposed to be at Central Church, our meeting place, by 12 noon. We were still eating at 12, and so we rushed to finish our food, left the plates on the table, grabbed our bags and hurried to our designated spot. We arrived just in time before Mr. Rochs start to worry.

We went to Manila Zoo, Port Santiago, Paco Cemetery. I will tell you all about these places we visited the next time we see each other, or my hands will get tired of writing everything. Some of the time, I felt a little dizzy as we get in and out of our transportation, in the hot weather, and then in and out of places. Everything was new and exciting, but we did not have enough time to really see more from each place.

From 6:00 pm we were given our own free time, ate at the Thames, and again went to Luneta, and this time Angkay Pitoy came with us. We walked around the park until 11:30 and were back at Central Church to depart at midnight. We were all tired, and so as soon as we settled on our seats, most of us immediately fell asleep.

We stopped in Dagupan for an early morning coffee, where we also played some music in the jukebox. The music made me think of you, my darling. We arrived in Anda at 7:30 am. I was asleep thirty minutes later. I did not wake up until 3 in the afternoon, skipping lunch altogether. This is my news about our enjoyable tour. Maybe if you were still in Asbury, you could have joined the field trip.

I did not tell you about this plan before because I thought my sister will not let me go. I told my father about the field trip and asked for his permission. He liked the idea, so he let me go. Anyway, you don't have to worry because we returned safely, and Angkay Tony was my companion during the trip.

This is letter is very long now. So long, my darling, until the next mail.

Forever loving you,

ECCaido

P.S. Here's our picture taken in Luneta. Though it's ugly, I hope that you will keep it as a remembrance of my class trip.

To you my love,

Due to my long vacation in the barrio (village), I was not able to respond to your letter. My dear, if ever I hurt you, I am so sorry for it. It was not my intention to do so. It's my eager desire to reply immediately, but sometimes time is quite selfish for us. But, don't you worry, my darling, no matter how far we are from each other, our thoughts connect us. Since I always think of you, that means we are connected, always.

Dear, because of your advice, I decided to cut my work hours at school. Besides, at home alone, I am already busy. You see, my classes are from 5:00 – 8:00 MWF and 4:00 – 8:30 TThS. Saturday morning, from 9:30 – 11:30, is PE. So, if I will still work very long hours, I don't know how I will cope with everything else. Thank you for your advice. I want to consider it.

I know that both of us are busy preparing for our future together. If once in a while I neglect to write to you, it's not because of anything but the busy schedule I have. So, I ask for your understanding when there's a delay in my letter getting to you. And as for me, sometimes I get frustrated, too, especially in waiting for when you could visit, but I do understand. You are very busy at work.

Let us keep our love strong enough to withstand the challenges we face. And remember me, your girl who prays for your safety wherever you are and wherever you go.

Bye for now. I will be waiting for you on Saturday with excitement. I hope you can come.

Always and forever,

LynCCaido

August 31, 1972

Dearest Roger,

I wonder why until now I have not received any message from you despite the news of flood that hit our area. I cannot have peace of mind and concentration in my studies until I know what is going on with you. Maybe it's because I care deeply, and I keep our sweet promises. I do hope you do the same and not let me wonder where you are or how you are doing.

'Ling, I have been busy with my studies that since Monday I have been going to bed really late. During the day, I am not able to read and study my lessons because there are so many things I have to do at home. Besides, my topsy turvy schedule does not help with all the work I have to do.

Below is my schedule. Bye for now. I am sincerely hoping for you to come here as soon as possible.

Yours till death,

Lyn

My schedule:

12:00 - 1:30	M/T	Pol. Science
5:00 – 6:30	M/W/F	Physics
7:30 – 9:00	T/Th/F	Physics
4:00 – 5:00	T/Th	English 5
5:00 – 6:00	T/Th	History 1
7:00 – 8:30	T/Th	Spanish
1:00 – 2:00	F	History 1
1:00 – 2:00	Sat	English 5
7:30 – 9:00	Sat	Phy. Educ.

Note: I am very quiet writing because everyone is asleep already.

Note: 'Ling - short for darling

October 19, 1972

Dearest Sweetheart,

I am so thankful for at last I received a message from you but those other two letters which you have mentioned before were totally lost. Before I proceed, let me extend my warmest greetings, and pray that you are safe and sound. Were you a victim of martial law? I mean, were you affected by it? I certainly hope and pray that you're not.

As for me, I am safe here. I think about your advice. It is my companion while I'm all alone. Your words are my consolation during these scary times.

Absence makes the heart grow fonder as they say. As much as I am fond of you even away, I would prefer that you are next to me. I know you are worried about me, but I promise that there are no temptations I cannot overcome for your sake. Besides, I don't look at others the way I looked at you. The truth is, I don't even "look" at all.

Dear, I hope you can understand why I gave those letters to you. Please keep it safe and let no one else read them. You are responsible for keeping them away from other curious eyes. You know me when I have a secret, I always share it with you.

May the good Lord bless and keep you till we meet again. Bye and be good always.

Forever and Always,

Lorelie

Note: Our semi-final is from October 19 to 21.

Dearest Roger,

Wishing you a joyous and happiest birthday. Are you celebrating with your friends?

On your very special day, my dear, I give you a special gift - a love that is true, specially and only for you.

Roger, I am very sorry for what had happened. The only thing I can say to you is to please act according to what you think is right. But don't you worry soon we will have the time when we can talk to each other, and hopefully, then we can discuss all of our plans for the future. I have not told them what you have told me, but "she" was the one who opened your letter, so she already knows your plans - I am sure!!! I will try to confer about this also with my father, but it will take me more time and courage. See, it is very hard on my part. I am not brave enough to face him and talk about it.

So long for now. Till we meet again, and I hope soon.

Forever loving you,

Lyn

Roger dearest,

After not hearing from you for what seems like forever, I thought that I am cast out of your mind and heart and can no longer forgive me. I am thankful for having someone who is understanding like you, dear.

I respect you, especially on how you honour and love me. So, from now on, I will try to be more understanding of you. Dear, you want to know what my decision is, whether you should accept the transfer or not. It's quite hard for me to be too far from you. If it is not necessary and it is not for your promotion, why should you take it? But if it is for your promotion, I prefer you to be in Baguio than in Zamboanga. The latter is considerably farther than the first. What happens when we are dying to see or missing each other very much? We have to travel a great distance, and both of us have limited free time.

If only I can help you, but I need more time to prepare for our future. Sometimes I think of not continuing my studies this coming year. I am considering taking up a vocational course instead. I consulted my Pa and sister about it, and they consented. They agree that it might be a better idea to follow, but I don't know if you will agree or disagree. I am thinking maybe dressmaking or tailoring or both.   I really want to study and finish what I started but it is taking so long. I would rather be with you sooner than later. I need your advice or suggestions.

Always take care. May the good Lord bless and keep you.

Dear, can you come on the 25th? If you can come home, please be here at 10 am. Bye...

Love,
Lyn

Roger dearest,

I am thrilled to know that you are "coming home." You will be closer to them and to me.

Roger, you asked me before why I am back in school despite our plans. Why? I am sure it is hard for you to accept it, but please think it over. What I am doing is not bad, is it? It is for our own good and also for our future, my darling. Am I not right?

You know, I have a noble purpose in pursuing my studies. Firstly, ever since I met you, you had implanted in my mind that I must strive hard for my education so that my Pa and sister's dream for me will not be in vain. Their dreams for me are my dreams, too, and I want them realized. Finishing my studies is what you have been telling me in the past. So, you see, I am also following your advice because it makes you happy. In the end, everyone is happy.

Secondly, you, your family, relatives, and friends as well, are all professionals. Won't you be proud if you're darling will also be like them and like you? A professional? I like the sound of that.

I want you to be proud of me, my darling.

Forever loving you,

Lyn

"Theirs was a beautiful story of friendship, patience, tremendous discipline, pride, understanding, hard work, devotion, true and enduring love. Their courtship started in 1971 and finally got married in August 1976. She wanted him to be proud of her. He wanted to support her dream of finishing her education.

Their marriage was blessed with two beautiful daughters, one of whom have recently found her own happily ever after and was recently married. The other is out on her world travel adventures. Perhaps one day, she'll bump into her prince charming on one of the exotic beaches she visits.

Roger passed away one month after they celebrated their 40th wedding anniversary. Lyn misses him every day, her first, her last, her one and only true love."

Feeling Red?!
Blush ♡

Hello:

After being friends for a while, I could not believe how nervous I was to go out on our first date. I thought it was strange to feel uneasy, unfocused, and unbelievably shaken with the idea of dating you after ceremoniously ignoring your invites. It is the opposite of how calm and comfortable I was when hanging out with you as friends. So, why should this be any different? I guess it's because I have chosen to see you in a different light - an intelligent man, ambitious, who works hard in following your dreams. You are strong but with a tender heart. You know what you want, and you are not the kind to be wasting time and playing games. Therefore, I believe that you wanting to get to know me more is intentional. I would be foolish not to give you, and a potential us, a try.

Days before our "official" date, I could not concentrate on work. Thoughts of *my friend* kept interrupting but always bringing a smile to my lips. And my nights? Well, I have found that there was no remedy to help an over-excited mind. So, I dream, fully awake, dancing with the fluttering of butterfly wings with great anticipation.

My special request to you was to have a relaxing date, where I can be me, and you can be you. I did not want to feel so conscious among people in an uptight place. You honoured that.

115

We had gone on walks before as friends where the ambience was befitting a romantic interlude for lovers. You couldn't resist the allure and offered your hands, so we may walk hand-in-hand. I laughed and flat out told you that you are not my boyfriend, and so why should I let you hold my hand. In my heart, I hoped then that I did not offend you.

Fast forward now to our dinner date. To start, you wanted to say a prayer of gratitude and blessing on the food and extended your hand to invite mine to join you. I hesitated for a second, "Is he being sneaky? Is he being spiritual?" I opted for the latter and graciously placed my right hand on top of your left hand. You squeezed it ever so gently as we closed our eyes and bowed our heads while an electric charge ran amok in my body as I fight to remain calm and collected in the outside.

I got home after what to me was such a romantic evening and asked myself, how can I be a grown-up woman and feel like a teenage girl, beaming from ear to ear, and now so infatuated with my friend that I could not wait for our next date. Patience is not one of my virtues, but I shall endure.

Thank you for being such a gentleman and spoiling me this evening.

With a delighted heart, xoxoxo

To my dearest Abu,

This card has been collecting all the dust on my desk for months... it's funny 'coz in the midst of work, my art sketch deadlines and aching bones, I finally get around to writing to you. Do you know that I actually miss calling you Abu? It seemed like ages ago. I can't believe it's going to be a year since I last saw you. So many things have changed already, but I guess missing you is one thing that won't.

I've been pretty busy lately 'coz my boss is on holiday, so I've been taking more shifts than usual. I can't wait for school to come so I can quit. Don't get me wrong - I love the shop and my boss. But too much of something is bad and I feel like it's becoming my life, to which it is not supposed to be. It seems like we won't be able to go home this August because Lola's transactions have been detained (as usual). It's okay. I guess it's not meant to be. Besides, I wouldn't want to give your No. 1 some competition when I visit you. I'm thinking of visiting Audz sometime soon and giving myself a well-deserved break. 'Coz, I know if I don't leave Vancouver soon, I'll never be able to quit my job. So, wish me luck.

So, what have you been up to? Oh, tell Ardic He can cross off my cuz on his list 'coz she got herself a man already. It was taking him a long time to pay her a visit. I guess you're buried with papers and tests again. Did I tell you I have nude art classes? Maybe someday I can show you my drawings. I have not attempted to draw the front yet though; I find it too complicated.

I miss you... but it's a different kind of miss though. I guess after two years, you get used to it. I still wish you were here. But I sort of accept the distance already. I still find it so hard to hold on, Abu. Like sometimes I can't help but wonder if you still feel the same, or if you're holding on, just for the sake of it. Or, if you've moved on without me. I can't blame you for these fears. For all I know, you must be having the same thoughts, too. And the truth is, I don't know how to make it better. I still love you and I think a part of me always will. But right now, a part of me will always wonder if you feel the same way. I know we've broken most of our "commitments," but I do hope you will always be open to me, as I always try to be with you.

I miss you. Give my love to the guys and your family. You take care there, ya hear?

I love you...

Katz

Dearest Abu,

It's hard for me to write to you; maybe b'coz until now, I'm still denying the fact that truly I am leaving you. But I guess it's too late for that now - it's blast-off time. Finally. The most awaited day has arrived. And I never knew it'd be this damn hard. I tried to find the right card for you — unfortunately, this is the best I could find. And although you are more than a friend to me, every line comes from the bottom of my heart. I'm going to miss you so much, Abu. I'll always remember everything we've gone through - from the big and silly fights we've had, to the crazy adventures we did... Mickey... your vanette, and my silly bloopers... Eden's house and the mosquitoes... bottled water... I could go on and on, but I guess the most important is all the things you taught me - like lowering my pride, being open to new beliefs, and getting rid of too much cynicism...

I know you deserve more than what I have given and that oftentimes I have failed to reach your standards, but I hope you know how much I truly love you. Letting you go must be the stupidest thing I'm ever gonna do. But knowing that in keeping you and yet not being able to love you as much as I can when I'm with you, would just be unfair to us both. After all, if we really are destined to be together, then fate will make a way.

There will be a lot of changes when I leave. There's no one to tease me anymore. I don't have you to clip fingernails for, or your feet I can tickle. No more drinking sessions together, or wild adventures to Baguio or Cavite, or shower-partner in the bathroom ... I guess only time will heal the loneliness and pain. There's one thing I want you to remember, Abu. Even if I leave and go away, you will never lose me. No matter how far away I may be, you will always be where it matters most - in my heart. Whatever changes may take place, you are always going to be my one and only Abu. And nothing can ever change that.

I don't want to make any promises. We don't know what the future may bring. But just in case we do go on our separate ways, don't forget that there was once this curly-haired girl who truly loved you - and will always will. I'll never forget you, Abu. You've been so much a part of me that no time or distance can take away. I will always hold on to the memory of you. Make the best out of life, okay? And remember that I will always love you...

"But even though we have to be apart, in a special way,
you'll still be there with me
because I'll think of you every time
I find something I think you'd enjoy.
I'll remember every detail
so I can share it with you when I see you again.

so even though it will be difficult to be away from you,
I'll take a part of you with me wherever I go
because you're too good a friend to leave behind."

Your Katz

Dearest Abu,

Would you believe I spent an hour in the card section for the perfect Valentine's card for you? And when I did, I just happened to have found this interesting card that speaks for itself.

I don't consider myself a very lucky person - in fact, there are times when I really believe I am cursed b'coz of all the failures I've gone through. But I guess you are my lucky charm. Not even the worst disaster or failure matters whenever I am reminded that you love me.

Abu, have you realized that in the 2 1/2 months we have been together, we were only able to celebrate two occasions: your birthday and Valentine's day? And yet those two days mean more than 10 years together. How I wish we could be together this Valentine's... At least I have that one Valentine's Day to cherish. And I would have rather had that one Valentine's Day with you than a lifetime without it.

I miss you, Abu. I am just dreaming of all the Valentine's Day when we'll be together for good. Don't you ever, ever forget that I love you.

Always,

Your Katz

P.S. Since I am back at school, I now have better ballpens.

I guess the card forgot to include... Only "Katz" belongs to Abu.

Subject: I'm back
Date: 13 April 1998
From: Katz
To: Abu

Hi. We heard your message in the answering machine. They all said that they miss you already and you're rich and that you're wasting money on an answering machine. We were away for the whole weekend. It was wonderful, and it felt heavenly. I think it was my longest time away from work. Now it's back to reality for me.

Wait... are you reading my emails? I actually sent you a dozen before this. I just want to make sure that you're getting all of them and that I'm not writing for nothing. Seattle was nice. We went shopping, but all I really bought was a big trunk for all my letters. Call me stupid, I don't care. It was just really cute. Abu, you won't believe this... just the other night, I had this really realistic dream about us. I was visiting CRC, and I was so excited to see you at last. But then when you saw me, you told me off, in no uncertain terms. And then I cried non-stop. I woke up, still crying. I thought it was true. It just made me realize that when that time comes - I mean, when you really decide to tell me to get lost, I don't think I'll be able to bear it.

I'd really love to call you right now, but then I know it's a Tuesday there and you have the car all to yourself. By the way, do they still use colour coding for

driving cars? Well, anyway, you're probably not home. I just hope you know how much I miss you...

Love you...

Katz

November 21, 1989

Dearest G,

Good day! How's Canada? I am always thinking of you; that's why I decided to write to you again. You know, my feelings for you grow stronger every day as I think of you. For a while, I have been contemplating about myself and my future. Time is ticking every second of the day, and it's pressuring me to be insecure. As we know it, our life here on earth is quite short, and we are only living in probationary time, so we need to make the most of it. We're getting older every day, and we cannot escape getting old. Procrastination is a sin that most people have that recognized yet. Most of us are still asleep, never waking up to the truth of life.

I, myself, is sinning because of this. Of course, I need to repent and open my eyes that I may see the realities of life. You know, most of my goals as a single person have already been fulfilled. With divine help, I was able to have success in my studies, career, my job, and my missionary work. I have nothing to ask for because God has been very good to me.

This time I have been praying to God that I may find my eternal companion and raise a family of my own that I may fulfill God's requirements of exaltation. It seems to me that I am failing, and I don't know why. I know there's a lot of things that I need to polish in myself. Perfection cannot be done overnight. Maybe God is punishing me or just giving me trials of my faith. I've got a lot of questions in my mind. But I don't need to worry, for I know that the Lord will provide a way that I may be able to fulfill His commandments. For sure, there's a lot of obstacles along the way. Like for instance, even though I have already found my prospective eternal companion, if she does not respond to my call, what shall I do? I can't do anything unless I rely on my faith.

Truly, I may say that being single is lonely and sad. I don't want to be single for the rest of my life and forever. Man's greatest joy is in the family, and that's my primary goal. I have to fulfil it that I may enjoy the life that God has blessed me.

Marriage is a part of this goal, and I'll marry someone who will accept me and love me for what and who I am. I have been courting you, G, because I have found in you the qualities that I've been looking in my future companion. Please accept me, and I'll marry you. Our decisions will mould our future. If we succeed, you'll be my queen, and I'll be your king, and we will live in eternal glory forever.

I love you.

Feeling Red?!
Blush!♡

My Darling Theresa,

I don't know what to say. I tried to phone on Sunday but couldn't get through. I hoped you would call me during the week but as yet no call.

I miss you very much and can't wait until September. I should arrive in Israel on Sunday, the 6th, probably at Haifa. I hope you will be able to meet me.

Can you also see about somewhere for me to stay? I will be there for two weeks.

My darling, I love you very much and wish we were together always. I think about you every day and carry your photo everywhere I go, and when I wake up in the morning, the first thing I see is your face. Oh, how I wish it were you I see next to me!

Every minute of every day I spend with you on my mind. Even when working, I cannot concentrate properly because I want only to think of you.

At the moment, I am something of a cripple. We were playing crickets, and I was going to catch the ball and had to dive forward, and I ended up taking the skin off my kneecaps. I now have bandages on both knees and am walking about like an old man. It's quite funny, really. At least all the lads find it funny as I can't even sit down and bend my legs.

When you phoned last Friday, you mentioned a decision about your studies, and you sounded worried. Don't you worry about anything. We will sort everything out in September. You'll see it will be OK.

Well, my love, I hope this letter finds you well. I love you and miss you.

All my love,

Glenn

24353896
CPL McLAUGHLAN
254 SIG SQN
UNFICYP
Nicosia, Cyprus

My Darling Theresa,

This is the third time I have tried to write this letter and each time, I run out of words. I just don't know the words to tell you how much I miss you. When you were here, I thought of you most of the day. Now it's even worse. I have this strange empty feeling inside. All my thoughts are with you.

I sit in my room every day and listen to your own tape, wishing you were here with me. Yet I know that in just a few weeks, we will be together again. How I look forward to that day!

During the four or five years since my wife left me, I thought I would never meet anyone else. Then, in a chance meeting with you, things seemed so different. It didn't happen at first. I can't really say when it did happen. All I know is how I feel about you. I wish I could say these things better, but I hope you can understand I love you.

Please don't misunderstand when I say that I know you have your own life. Things that are important to you, your studies and your life in Israel. If you wish to carry on with that, well, I can understand. I will hate it, but I love you too much to make you give them up. I want you to be happy at all costs, whatever it may mean to me.

Well, my love, I hope you can read this and understand what I'm trying to say.

I love you forever and can't wait to see you again in September. Bye for now.

Love,

Glenn

11 August 1981

My Darling Theresa,

I hope this letter finds you well and in good spirits. I wish I could say the same about myself. I miss you very much. What makes it worse is the fact that I have not heard from you for three weeks.

I have tried Mr. Austria's number every Sunday, but you are never there. I wish you would phone or write. Mr. Austria told me last Sunday you have moved and don't know where to. If I don't know where you are, how can I come to Israel in September? Unless I hear from you, I shall cancel my holiday. What would be the point of it if I were not with you?

My darling, if anything has changed between us, please oh please, tell me. I can't bear not knowing.

I love you very much more than anything in the world and will do anything to keep that love alive. Please write or phone and tell me what is happening.

My darling, there is a record in England by the "Climax Blues Band." I wish you could hear it. It seems so apt about the way I love you. You came from miles away to love me and make me happy. If I lose you, I don't know what is left for me to do.

Last Wednesday, Dave and Eve had a party at their house. Dave, me and Nick went. It was quite nice, but I would have preferred it if you had been there. I felt very sad seeing Dave and Eve so happy together while we are so far apart.

My darling, I want you to know everything I have said or written about my love for you comes from the bottom of my heart. I hope someday to make you my wife so I can tell you every day just how much I love you. I know this sounds corny, but it's how I feel. I miss you.

Well, my love, it is now 6:30 and no phone call. I sit here every day and wait to see if there will be a call and when it doesn't come, I go to the club and usually end up drunk. Sometimes me and Dave go downtown, but I don't enjoy it because it only reminds me of when you and I went for a drink to the Odessia.

Well, my darling, I am sorry if this is a sad letter, but that is how I feel. I can't smile while we are apart. I love and miss you so. Please please write or phone.

All my everlasting love,

Glenn

My Darling Theresa,

I received your letter yesterday and have read it almost constantly since. How can I tell you how much I love you? I need you so much. God! I wish you were here with me. I could show you just how much I love you.

I wish I had known about all the problems you had when you returned to Israel. If I had, I would not have let you go.

Thank you for the gift. I will treasure it always. I only wish you were here to give it to me yourself.

When Dave spoke to Eve, he told me something about you coming back with her. It was all very confusing, and I tried not to look forward to it, but I was upset when I found out it was all a misunderstanding on Dave's part.

Well, never mind, I should be in Israel in the second week of September. I don't know if I will fly or come by boat but will tell you when I have booked.

Things here are much the same. Nick is away for two weeks' holiday with his family, so I have a lot of work, but all I think about is you and work very slowly.

I love you.

Well, on Wednesday you will phone me. How I long for these calls just to hear your voice again. You don't know what it means to me.

Well, my love, I will finish this letter now and post it in the morning. It takes about 2 weeks for you to receive it, so when you get this, we will have only 2 or 3 weeks before we are together again.

All my love,

Glenn

P.S. I love and miss you very much.

My Darling Theresa,

I am sorry if I was quiet yesterday when I left you, but I was so upset at leaving you. If I had said what I felt, I would have cried all the way back to Cyprus.

I was so choked up trying not to cry I could hardly speak, but I was so glad to see you stood at the window after we had said goodbye. If only to have you laugh at my sore back.

I miss you, my darling, and wish you had come back with me. I know I can wait until December for you to come to Cyprus, it will seem like a life-time, but I would wait anyway. I only hope you can wait. Nothing will ever change about the way I feel about you, and when you reply to this letter, I want to know if you meant what you said about getting engaged in December.

I was serious when I asked you. I only hope you were. I LOVE you very much, and I want to spend the rest of my life, showing you just how much I do love you. Leaving you in Haifa was one of the hardest things I have ever done, and I don't ever want to leave you again.

Well, my darling, what else can I say? Send my best wishes to all your friends I met in Israel. They are all very nice people. Oh, by the way, my back is much better today, although it is still quite painful to sit down and as yet, no one has made a comment as to how I received it.

My darling, I love and miss you very very much and wait for the day we are together again, and also for the day we are married and are, at last, together forever.

All my everlasting love,

Glenn

P.S. I really do love and miss you from the bottom of my heart.

21 September 1981

My Darling Theresa,

Well, my love, I hope your first day at work went OK. I am afraid mine did not. I was very busy and could only think of you.

I really wish you had come to Cyprus with me. I hate having to be parted, but they do say absence makes the heart grow fonder if it is possible for me to love you more than I already do.

I saw Eve yesterday (Sunday) and passed on the messages. She wanted your phone number as well so she will probably be phoning you.

I want to tell you that I honestly did enjoy my holiday with you. I know we didn't seem to get on, and we argued, but my darling, it was all just misunderstandings. I only wanted to be with you. I LOVE YOU AND MISS YOU VERY VERY MUCH.

Please take care of yourself and come to me in December. I am waiting for the day we are together again so please come as soon as you can.

All my everlasting love goes out to you, my darling.Bye for now.

Love,

Glenn

P.S. I hope you believe me when I say I LOVE YOU 'cos it's true.

My Darling,

Before I came to Israel, I felt myself opening up, willing to let my feelings show for the first time in years since my wife left me. I have never let myself get even remotely involved with anyone until I met you. I thought you were different. I knew I could trust you with my love. I knew you would not let me down and hurt me again.

Then the bomb dropped. You told me you did not wish to marry me. I am sorry for acting the way I did, but I could not help myself. You see, it was all happening again like a bad dream. It was all happening, although in different circumstances, it was just the same.

Then you had a change of heart. Why I don't know. I can only hope it was not out of sympathy or pity because I can live without both. That is no reason to marry someone. The only real reasons for marriage are love, respect, and deep knowledge that this is what we both want. Any other way is a lie, and I couldn't live on lies.

I do love you and want to spend the rest of my life with you, but not unless that is what you want also. I will not post this letter but will wait until we are together to let you read it.

You will probably ask why. Well, I have said for years I lived almost in isolation from any relationship. I was scared and didn't want to be hurt, not the kind of hurt like before.

So I keep things to myself, only this time, I want you to know. Yet my natural defence is not to tell you, not to say anything.

I love you, my darling.

Glenn

18 December 1981

My Darling Theresa,

Well, love, it's nearly Christmas now, and I am missing you more than ever. I understand why you cannot come out before and can only wait until you do. I love you and miss you very much.

Now I have to confess that the last letter I sent you, I never posted because it wasn't a very nice letter. I was depressed and feeling sorry for myself and should never have written it. I realize that just as I was about to post it and I tore it up.

The reason is not important. What is very important to me is that I don't lose you. If I did, I don't know what I would do. I love you so very much.

Well, my darling, I am very busy just now. I am in charge of the Mercury Club and have to organize a Dinner Dance in the Hilton Hotel, and this is taking up most of my spare time. I seem to be on the go all the time. It is very hard to get things done because all I really want to think about is when you come over here to me. That is the most important thing.

Thank you, my darling, for the birthday card. It really cheered me up. I am only sorry you could not get through on the phone, but at least I know you were thinking of me cos I was thinking of you. I didn't go for that meal cos the lads all backed out, not that I was bothered. I got a bottle of wine and sat in my room all night and decided that when you are here, then we will go for a meal just the two of us and celebrate my birthday, Christmas, and the fact that you and I are together again. Well, my love, at the moment, I am trying to get a phone call to you, but if I don't get you, I will try every day until I get through.

I wish you the very merriest of Christmases and promise that you will not be out of my thoughts for even one second until we are together again.

All my everlasting love,

Glenn

P.S. I love you and only you. See you soon. Bye.

My Darling Theresa,

Well, love, it is now the 21st of January, 10:30 in the evening. Things aren't going too well. I am full of cold and keep making mistakes on the drill square. I don't know. The harder I try, the more mistakes I make. We go on a 2-day exercise on Thursday. It is going to be very cold.

But not long now before I come home. I never realize just how much I could miss you and Rachel. If by any chance, I do fail this course, I will never come back and try again. It's not worth being away from home.

I don't think I will get to Bradford before the end of the course. I really have so much work to do.

Anyway, damn the course. I will give it my best try, and if that's not good enough, well, we will be ok.

I am sorry I had to get more money from you, but it just goes so fast. I have only been to the mess a couple of times through the week and then not till late, about nine-thirty. But you have to get out occasionally and relax.

I am sending Marivic's results back as I can't understand them. You will have to explain when I get back. Can you see John Phillips and tell him to let me know if Kieth is still on the next course as I would like to leave my webbing and sleeping bag here with the SQMS.

If Kieth is on the next course, he can leave his kit in Germany and get it from the SQMS here. The kit I will leave has:

Sleeping bag
Webbing
Tin helmet

Well, love, I will close now. I am sorry if this letter seems a little sad, but I am just tired. I am sure everything will be ok. All my love. I miss you very much. Give Racheal a kiss for me. I will save a big one for you when I get home.

I miss and love you very much.

All my love,

Glenn

P.S. Ask John to let me know about the kit.

P.P.S. When you send the money at the end of the month, can you send it in pounds as I cannot get to the bank to change it.

Feeling Red?
Blush ♡

Unable to sleep, restive and alone,
I spoke on the phone,
to a bonny we lass,
with dimples in a class that is hers alone.

Of all my esteemed friends,
the one I like to be with best,
Is that precious dear lady
who resides in the west.

I would journey many a mile,
just to experience her exquisite sweet smile.
Her much sought hug and warm kiss,
tantamount to Heaven-sent bliss.

I live with a hope, however remote,
that it could be, the treasured dear lady
might care to eventually
share travel with me.

Dear Friend,

I feel that I have been reasonably fortunate in life, but meeting you has been among my most delightful experience.

I trust my bit of doggery will not prove to be offensive.

My best personal regards to you.

Friday, 23 July 1999

My dearest,

Wednesday evening, I was watching the late news in a rather desultory fashion. The fact is I was thinking of you and wondering if I might be fortunate enough to again see you, when, as if by magic, you appeared before me speaking of illegal immigrants, arriving by ship.

Only one week ago, you placed your small soft hand in mine as together, we explored Ottawa. You cannot imagine my happiness and, indeed, the pride I felt being with you. As I looked into your smiling face, I felt that you were happy, too.

If, as I have read, "nothing happens by coincidence," then I had reaped a fantastic harvest when you sewed on one small button which had become detached from my jacket. I glimpsed you on that Vancouver to Ottawa flight. I knew at once that I must meet you, but how? Was the loose button an act of Providence, or did it happen by chance?

You state in your letter that there is much that I do not know about you. There are also certain things that you do not know about me. One is that I am not as modest as I should like to think. That is the reason that I am forwarding a copy of the 2nd June Hansard to you.

We do, I think, have a number of things in common. We enjoy gardening, things of beauty and the good life. We are both winners, accustomed to and fond of achieving our goals. If there is anything that I can do to help you succeed, I am most anxious to assist.

This has turn out to be longer than first anticipated. It is my earnest hope that we shall again see each other in November. Meanwhile, please take care. You are very beautiful and extremely precious.

Yours as aye,

A

P.S. I did enjoy the paintings on Sunday, although I fear I know little about art. I do have a miniature signed portrait by Van Loo of Lord Darnley, second husband of Mary Queen of Scots. Also, I have a brooch which once belonged to that unfortunate Queen. Mary's own hair, finely woven, forms the background for the gold-rope coat-of-arms.

How I wish that you could be my dining companion this evening! - A

Monday, September 13, 1999

My love,

Many thanks for the photos – I just love that cowgirl!

I am enclosing a few items of interest: stickers for the young ones, 2 articles on the Chinese boat people (one of them by your favourite columnist) and a useful piece on "de-mutualization" which you may find helpful. I received it from my stockbroker.

I, too, find a long-distance relationship to be less than satisfying. I, too, would like to be with you every day, to buy the groceries, take out the garbage, have dinner on the balcony, dance in the moonlight, spend holidays together, help pay the bills, help you raise those 2 precious children who mean so much to you and, you may find it hard to believe, who also means a great deal to me. I love you all very dearly and want very much to share our lives together.

On Sunday, my son and I went to the football game – it was a beautiful summery day, a lot of fun and the Alouettes clobbered Hamilton 52 – 19; even there I was thinking how nice it would be in a few years to take the older one to football and other sporting activities and the younger one when he's a little older.

151

Not a single day passes without you and the little ones sneaking into my thoughts. I get excited at the thought of sharing your bed every night, of cuddling you and making love to you.

You may recall that when I first raised the subject of marrying you some years ago, I was even prepared to start a family with you.

I so enjoy being with you and, like you, would dearly love to spend much more time together. As you may have observed, at this time, I am not ready to leave Montreal. However, that is not to say that I will never be ready to leave Montreal. As you so well know, Montreal is in my blood, it's part of my being. So much of me is invested in Montreal that it will require a genuine uprooting to remove me – and you, my darling, enjoy the honour and the privilege of being the one person who has come closest to succeeding, and you may yet do so. I am not being facetious – I think you know how much I would have to leave behind. When I tell you that I agonize over this decision, I mean that literally.

Whether I write to you, phone you or email you, you are <u>always</u> in my thoughts. Even if you don't hear from me, you are in my thoughts.

I know what a challenge and a chore (albeit a delightful challenge and chore) it is bringing up the children by yourself. I meant so much to be there to help you. There is so much I can do to help raise and educate them.

I miss you when we're apart and so look forward to our next meeting. I'm planning to come to Vancouver sometime in mid-October. If the opera is performing at that time, so much the better.

As always and forever,
My deepest love

C

Hi, Beautiful!

I tried to get you a sable coat, but they didn't have your size – instead, I'd like you to bring some perennial seeds of love to plant in your garden and which will continue to bloom for years to come. You might even dedicate a small corner of your cherished garden to us and our love.

Whenever I'm with you, I feel like showering you with kisses... or is it kissing you in the shower. Hmmmm, now that I think about it... I'm rather partial to both prospects.

I love you, darling and would love to embrace you right now.

With much love and affection for you.

Au revoir, sweetheart.

C

September 1, 1999

Dear Woman of Wonder with the classy chassis,
   Sweetheart, Darling, Jewel,

How does one do this? Do you remember the three fortune cookies I opened before coming out there? Well, I found them, and here they are. They are in the order I first read them. As you can probably guess, ordinarily, I am the least superstitious, most skeptical, if not downright cynical when it comes to such things. But in this particular case, I am fully prepared to suspend all previous attitudes and claim total, lifelong belief in fortune-tellers (and their cookies).

So, here's #1 – "Sometimes a stranger can bring great meaning to your life. Lucky Numbers 8, 11, 15, 19, 26, 40."

True, you were not a total stranger at that point. In fact, I had already kissed you, albeit lightly and politely, but it counted for me. I had some idea of what it would be like to have you in my arms. I had sensed your warmth and an oh-so brief zing of excitement.

And so to #2 – "You will become more passionate and determined about your convictions. Lucky Numbers 14, 15, 18, 24, 36, 45" - and how!!!

Number 3 is, perhaps, the least easy to present. At first sight, it smacks of conceit and brashness – not

155

characteristics I deliberately cultivate. But in a deeper sense, maybe I am approaching a point I have been preparing for over many years. I have wanted to make a commitment but did not know what to. Sailing and sailboats have been the focus, with people and personal relationships representing distraction.

I want to be immersed in things. Usually, this represents a threat or at least an inconvenience to others. My solution has been to stay aloof and keep my own counsel. Suddenly I find myself looking into the eyes of a beautiful, adventurous, gutsy woman, who seems to be saying anything I can do would be fine by her.

Perhaps this is all a bit much from one fortune cookie, but – what the heck!

3 – "Your self-confidence shines and makes a great impression on others. Lucky Numbers 5, 14, 20, 25, 26, 33."

I will not go into the circumstances by which I found the CD. All I ask is that you find the right moment to listen to the first track. I cannot begin to describe my feelings when I heard it. For a moment, I was back on the balcony, looking at the moon, holding you. I speak no Italian. I had no prior knowledge of the singer or song. Yet instantly, the sound summoned an intense feeling in me. I knew it was something of significance, but what? Whatever he was saying, he was saying for me. Perhaps music is the universal language after all. How can an unintelligible noise capture and convey emotion so poignantly? It sounded exactly as I felt – as I still feel. Then, of course, I read the title...

The necklace sort of goes on from there. Think of every little bead as a kiss. Each is precisely placed, perfectly spaced, delicious little kisses...

And careful with the newspaper packing. I'm not sure J and S know I took it, but I knew you wanted it and will probably take better care of it than they would. Motto: "Every day deserves one juicy rationalization..."

Hoping you find some joy and peace in these words; they are a valiant effort but fall far short of my feelings for you at this moment.

Rx

Dearest,

Your arriving company got me off the phone, so I could write to you at last. I have read and re-read the "how will you change?" letter. I'm actually not expecting to change very much, and if I do, I'm sure it will be for the better. One good thing about maturity is the perspective one has of hindsight. Besides, I had this fortune cookie right as your letter arrived...

"You should be able to undertake and complete anything. Lucky Numbers 27, 28, 32, 34, 38, 43." – need I say more?

It would be inappropriate of me to brag or overstate my abilities, so I won't. Suffice it to say, I'm not doing this for a lark or for some young flesh (say hi to P for me please). Perhaps I should qualify that with a "just," i.e. I'm not doing this just for some young flesh – unless you want to include some young warm putty people as well.

I hope I am above all else a kind and generous person, slow to anger and quick to smile. There have been quite a few who have sought to corral me for their own purposes, and I suppose I have been happy enough to let them. After all, I have had a wonderful life, far more rewarding than I could ever have imagined. I like to think people are better off knowing me and having me around.

I know it's jumping the gun, but the boys need a man friend, someone to teach them how to be men – not copies of their father. (I don't mean to degrade him, especially in their eyes). They do need some alternatives though, and perhaps I can help them achieve some balance.

Richard Burton was talking about Elizabeth Taylor... something along the lines of, "she rushes to me like a wave to a rock, crashing upon me in thousands of ways, submerging me, leaving me gasping..." If ever I met a wave of a woman, it would be you. And I would be your rock. Each of us will be changed by our meeting. You will run through every fissure and fault of my being. I will cause you to explode upwards, making a rainbow of your spray in the sun.

A brief but lovely moment before you gather together again and run from me to do what waves do without rocks. And the rock stands firm and resolute – well enough to be a rock alone until she comes again.

In dealing with sick, elderly people, one can be struck by how overwhelmed they are by all the "what if's" they perceive. My attempt to lessen their burden centers on one thing at a time. Don't waste time and energy on "what if's" because when the actual situation reveals itself, you will need all your strength and courage to deal with it. So, let it happen then deal with it. I don't think one should give advice unless one is prepared to act the same way.

There is also something to do with the purity of the heart. Not being a religious chap, I have come to the purity of the heart as my ultimate motivational goal. You are welcome to me, take what you need, use me well. This is my love.

"Traveling more often is important for your health and happiness. Lucky Numbers 11, 12, 13, 14, 16, 21."

Rx

Feeling Red?! Blush ♡

My dear, darling. How are you? I am back to doing the things that I'm very uncomfortable doing, but you love, so I'm doing it because it's Valentine's Day. It's your day, and I'm going to do everything that you want me to do. Firstly, I want to thank you for the parcel, beautiful parcel addressed to me from you. I have not opened it, but I want to thank you for it, whether it's a note or a card or whatever it is. I am thankful, and I appreciate you for being the kind of person that you are. Since I met you, I have been very happy. You've been loving. You know, we have had our ups and downs, but the love has been consistent. So, I really appreciate you today, and I celebrate you. I am going to have a very good meal, and I will toast to you. It's not going to be alcoholic since you don't like alcohol, but I got something celebratory. I'm celebrating us. I'm celebrating you with a bottle of sparkling juice. I will have some bubbly with no alcohol, just for you.

I thank you for everything you've done in my life. I thank you for taking a chance on us. I thank you for overcoming all the prejudices that you thought affected us. I thank you for overcoming your fears and for just giving of yourself. I do hope I make you happy and just so you know, I spent around the first 25 minutes trying to get that perfect song that explains what I think about you. I have been retaking it, and now I have a hoarse voice. I have been speaking a lot today, too, so it wasn't coming out as well as I wanted, but I really want to please you, so

I did it over and over again until I got something possibly nice and possibly will cheer you up. And possibly will talk about what I feel about you.

I love you, Babe, Happy Valentine. I'm sorry that I couldn't express it with a gesture of grandeur, extremism, or whatever it is that people do, but you know where my heart is, and you know that I'm very happy and that I love you. I am sending your lovely video gift. I hope you like it. It may not be sung beautifully, but you know that it comes from my heart, and those words, hopefully, resonates with what I feel about you. Alright, Sweetie, Happy Valentine.

Note: This was the song sang by the gentleman himself (by Shania Twain).

You got a way with me
Somehow you got me to believe
In everything that I could be
I've gotta say, you really got a way
You got a way it seems
You gave me faith to find my dreams
You'll never know just what that means
Can't you see, you got a way with me
It's in the way you want me
It's in the way you hold me
The way you show me just what love's made of
It's in the way we make love

You got a way with words
You get me smiling even when it hurts
There's no way to measure what your love is worth
I can't believe the way you get through to me
It's in the way you want me
It's in the way you hold me
The way you show me just what love's made of
It's in the way we make love

Oh, how I adore you
Like no one before you
I love you just the way you are
It's in the way you want me
Oh, it's in the way you hold me
The way you show me just what love's made of
It's in the way we make love
It's just the way you are

Blush! ♡

If you would like to share your unpublished love letters
for the next collection, please email me:

feelingpinklove@gmail.com

Feeling Blue?

JUMP!

Me-An Laceste

Feeling Pink? L♥VE!

Me-An Laceste

Manufactured by Amazon.ca
Bolton, ON

10968578R00101